A GUIDE TO
MYSTIC FAERIE
TAROT

About the Author

BARBARA MOORE IS a Certified Tarot Reader through the American Tarot Association and has spoken at tarot conferences around the United States. Her articles on tarot have appeared in several tarot publications and in Llewellyn Publications' *New Worlds of Mind and Spirit* magazine. She has also sat on the *Tarot Journal* editorial board. Barbara's own education in the tarot has been and continues to be broad and enlightening. She has studied under renowned tarot scholars Mary K. Greer and Rachel Pollack, and she has taught the tarot to all manner of would-be tarot readers. She has also written *The Gilded Tarot Companion* (part of Ciro Marchetti's best-selling *Gilded Tarot* kit) and *What Tarot Can Do for You*, both published by Llewellyn.

www.mysticfaerie.com

About the Artist

LINDA RAVENSCROFT IS a self-taught British artist whose beautifully detailed faerie and fantasy images can be seen all over the world from fine-art prints to exclusive giftware and faerie art books, such as *The Art of Faerie* and *The World of Faerie*. Linda's own book, *How to Draw and Paint Fairies: A Step-by-Step Guide to Fairy Art* (Watson-Guptill, 2005), has been a great success, having been translated into several languages and selling worldwide.

Linda also has a website dedicated to her art:

www.lindaravenscroft.com

A GUIDE TO
MYSTIC FAERIE
TAROT

≫ *Barbara Moore* ≪

TAROT CARD ARTWORK BY
LINDA RAVENSCROFT

Llewellyn Publications
WOODBURY, MINNESOTA

FIRST EDITION
Eighth Printing, 2018

Book design by Rebecca Zins
Cover design by Ellen Dahl
Cover illustration and interior cards © 2006 Linda Ravenscroft
Other interior artwork from Dover Publications (from *Old-Fashioned Floral Designs CD-ROM and Book,* © 1990, 1999), *Art Explosion* (©2004 Nova Development), and *Desk Gallery* (©1994 Zedcor, Inc.)

Llewellyn is a registered trademark of Llewellyn Worldwide Ltd.

. . . .

ISBN 13: 978-0-7387-0921-5
ISBN 10: 0-7387-0921-2

This book is a component of the *Mystic Faerie Tarot* kit,
which consists of a boxed set of 78 full-color cards,
a tarot bag, and this perfect-bound book.

. . . .

Llewellyn Worldwide does not participate in, endorse, or have any authority or responsibility concerning private business transactions between our authors and the public.

All mail addressed to the author is forwarded but the publisher cannot, unless specifically instructed by the author, give out an address or phone number.

Any Internet references contained in this work are current at publication time, but the publisher cannot guarantee that a specific location will continue to be maintained. Please refer to the publisher's website for links to authors' websites and other sources.

Llewellyn Publications
A Division of Llewellyn Worldwide Ltd.
2143 Wooddale Drive
Woodbury, MN 55125-2989

www.llewellyn.com

For Jessica, a remarkable young woman who beautifully blends the mystical and the practical into her own special faerie magic, and to Lisa, for her unerring encouragement and deep understanding of the 10 of Cups. Thank you, Linda, for creating such lovely art and giving me something so magical to write about. Special thanks to Becky for clarifying and polishing my writing and for designing such an enchanting book.

〝B. M.

For my faerie muse and model daughter Vivien; also her friends Lizzie, Myles, and Dom, who only charged £1 each for their modeling skills.

For little Charlotte, who will always shine brightly in our hearts.

Special thanks to my long-suffering husband, John; Mum and Dad, my best critics; my sister Vivien and little Matty; dear Barbara, who has translated my images so beautifully into words; my friends at Macouti—Mel, Helen, Zoe, and Nome, but especially Trish (my Star) and Stigg (who is an excellent King); also Angi, Merni, and Silas at the Duirwaigh Gallery.

〝L. R.

Contents

ARTIST'S NOTES

I was born in 1963 and am a very typical Pisces, always preferring to live in a dream world, a world which I have painted ever since I can remember and one which as a child I could retreat to whenever things became tough. I still pay regular visits to my dream world, though with a lot more of the real world thrown in ...

It's where I go to paint.

I live in the beautiful county of Cheshire, England (famous for its Cheshire Cat, of course), with my long-suffering husband, John, daughter Vivien, and numerous pets.

My home is situated near a very small wood, which is a constant source of inspiration to me.

ARTIST'S NOTES

I use many mediums for my paintings, though my favourite has to be watercolour. I love the gentleness of the colours and the way the colours blend.

My inspiration comes from many sources. I rely mostly on my dreams and inner feelings, as I have done since I was a child, along with my love of nature, instilled within me from an early age by my parents and their wonderful tales of myths and legends which they would share with me at bedtime.

Now as an adult with more experience of the world, I am influenced by artists from the past, such as Alphonse Mucha and William Morris, and the era in which they lived and worked. I also have a fascination for the supernatural and unexplained; all of these elements help to fire my imagination and enable me to create my images.

The idea of the faerie folk or earth spirits— call them what you will—dates back as far as time itself. To me, they represent the natural world we live in, and whether you believe in the fae or not, I feel that they have a place in our modern-day society even more now than they ever did in the past.

ARTIST'S NOTES

It's time to look at our beautiful world and take stock of our feelings and behaviour towards our fellow man, time to open our eyes to see what harm we are doing.

I find it easier to translate some of my feelings into my work. Ironically, the sort of feelings that make you feel powerless to do anything about can be turned into the most enchanting images. These are usually some of my larger, more complicated paintings, each one containing my messages of hope and perhaps a gentle reminder to take care of the world and each other.

Most of my images are serene and benign, although we all have a darker, more passionate side waiting to emerge. After all, we are only human.

I truly believe that we all have a little bit of faerie magic within our hearts, helping us to make the right decisions within our everyday lives; we just have to look for it.

I painted this deck with inspiration and love for our own mystic garden, this wonderful world of ours. The stories within the cards are there to ask questions about the way we live and treat each other and our fellow creatures. I hope that

ARTIST'S NOTES

this deck brings hope and good fortune to all who own and use it.

Shine brightly and live your dreams,

Linda

INTRODUCTION

Welcome to the Garden

ARE YOU READY for an adventure? When you enter the realms of the *Mystic Faerie Tarot*, you will explore the enchanted world of the fae. What kind of journey will you experience?

Imagine yourself in a long-forgotten garden. It is overgrown and untended yet beautiful and alluring. You are drawn in and compelled to explore. A splash of color here, an intriguing shape there. A soft leaf just asks to be touched. A spicy floral scent captures your attention. You hear a quiet sound, perhaps a bee flitting from bloom to bloom. You hardly know where to look first. You walk toward a section of purple flowers.

As you move closer, you notice a path partially hidden by foliage. Peering down the path through the variegated green leaves obscuring your view, you notice sunlight reflecting and bouncing off something. Trying to focus, you think you see a small bird, its wings gently stirring the air. But it doesn't look like any bird you've ever seen. The rich colors and graceful movement are too magical to be a bird. Do you follow it?

The faeries of *Mystic Faerie Tarot* will help guide your way through the garden. The garden is really your life, and the tarot can help you find your path. You can use it to explore possibilities so that you can make better decisions. If you make better decisions, you can create the life you long to live. You can find ways to achieve your heart's desires. You can figure out how to best realize your dreams. As you go along, you will discover things about yourself, too. You can learn your greatest strengths and how to use them. You will see your weaknesses or parts of yourself, your behavior, and your way of thinking that you don't like, that you'd like to change. When you identify these, you can weed them out and transform yourself.

INTRODUCTION

And you can, if you are willing, face your fears and find the courage to overcome them.

Is this too much to ask of a deck of cards, however lovely? Not really. People have used the tarot for decades, maybe centuries, as a means of self-discovery. The tarot has, throughout the years, helped many seekers find what they were looking for.

This book will serve as a map to help you navigate and use the elements within the *Mystic Faerie* cards. First, you'll find out what a tarot deck is and why this one is so special. Then you'll be introduced to all the cards. Finally, you will learn how to do a reading for yourself.

The faerie garden is truly a wondrous place. Explore it to find the magic and wonder in yourself and in your life. May every step of your journey be enchanted.

CHAPTER 1

Why Tarot?

THE TAROT HAS been used for fortunetelling, for people to try to see what the future holds. But this is not the best use of the cards, for the future is not set in stone, and you do have the power to make your own fortune. You can use the tarot to see what happened in the past that is affecting your present. You can see what is happening now that you should be aware of. And you can, it is true, see what the probable future holds . . . but that future is always being remade with every moment that passes. Within those moments, you can make decisions that will change the future.

Why is the tarot so effective? What makes
the tarot different from any other deck of cards?
The tarot is not a random collection of pretty
pictures and odd names. It is a carefully designed
deck that covers all aspects of the human experience—from major events like graduating college
to everyday happenings like having an argument
with a loved one. It can even show personality
traits of yourself or of other people in your life.

How does it do that? A tarot deck has seven-
ty-eight cards divided into three main parts: the
Major Arcana, the Minor Arcana, and the court
cards. Each of these sections covers a different
aspect of life. *Arcana* means "mystery" or "secret."

The twenty-two cards of the Major Arcana
are identified by a name (like the Magician,
the Empress, Death, or the Sun) and a Roman
numeral. The images on the Major Arcana show
the major events in life. They serve as signposts
defining where you are on your path. You can also
use them for insight about what to expect when
facing these major events.

The Minor Arcana is made up of forty cards.
They are divided into four suits—Wands, Cups,

Swords, and Pentacles—with an ace through ten in each suit. Each card is labeled with its number and suit. The Minor Arcana show events and situations that we face in everyday life. Each of the suits focuses on a different part of everyday life, such as career, emotions, problems, and money. While they lack the star appeal of the Major Arcana, the Minor Arcana do make up the majority of your life. Don't make the mistake, as some do, of thinking they are second-rate cards.

There are sixteen court cards, with a king, a queen, a knight, and a page for each of the suits in the Minor Arcana. Each card, like the Minors, is labeled with its title and suit. These cards show both the various people in our lives and the different aspects of our own personality.

Because of the tarot's unique design, it defines all aspects of the human experience incredibly well. The tarot consists of more than words, more than card names and simple interpretations that cleanly and conveniently label these experiences—for life is anything but clean and convenient. The words do provide a framework and basic understanding, but the pictures on the cards are essential to the tarot's power. It's when you look at the pictures that the magic happens.

Often when you think you don't know what to do, you really do. But fear or logic or what other people think gets in the way. The tarot can help you get past those things and find the answers in your heart. To get to those answers, you need a bridge, a place where your heart can communicate with your mind. Sometimes this place is called the imagination—where you can entertain different possibilities. The pictures on the tarot cards create a connection between your conscious mind and your inner self, a space where you can access the answers that reside in your heart. When you are in this realm, you can see things that normally are hidden. Possibilities and answers that seemed so elusive before are now more accessible.

The names of the cards and the structure of the deck into sections are orderly and rational. They are the language of your conscious mind and help it feel more comfortable. The pictures are the language of your inner self. When you put the words and pictures together, you have the tarot—a perfect bridge between your mind and your heart. When doing your readings and interpreting the cards, remember that the words in this book are here to help you—though they will not have all the answers. To get the complete story, you must look carefully at the pictures and let your mind play with the images. Pay attention to things that stand out. The thoughts and feelings that are triggered by the images may very well mean more to you than the words in this book.

As amazing as the tarot is, there is something different and more powerful when faeries are added, especially when the faeries inhabit a world created by Linda Ravenscroft. While the faeries she paints are without question intensely beautiful, they are more than that, in both style and substance. Stylistically, she presents complex and compelling images that provide not just a bridge but also a veritable playground for your imagination. Her work invites you to explore the depths of the faerie garden and to interact with the beings inhabiting it. It more than invites; it compels. Linda's art creates a luminous portal that more fully draws you into a realm of otherworldliness so that you can let go and be open to all possibilities.

WHY TAROT?

If her only achievement were stylistic, that would be quite enough to set *Mystic Faerie* apart from other tarot decks. However, she brings deeper substance as well. While creating this deck, Linda said, "I believe that we all have a little bit of faerie magic within our hearts helping us to make the right decisions in our lives. I hope that my paintings help people to stop and think a little, yet still find some comfort and hope within their everyday lives. I have always associated the fae hand in hand with nature, guardians of the world ... the images I am trying to portray are those of a wise, caring, proud race of people, all of whom have blood ties to nature in one way or another."

The *Mystic Faerie Tarot* is inhabited by faeries who are part of the natural world in a way we can only hope to be. We are separated by that which makes us human—our self-consciousness and self-awareness. Yet it is our heart's desire to be connected and in balance with nature. At a psychological level and probably even more so at the soul level, the desire to be connected with the universe is what drives us. Our religious and spiritual beliefs and our stories and myths all speak to this desire.

Alas, we cannot fully connect with nature in the same way as the fae. But we can achieve a sense of balance and flow with the universe. During the times in our lives when we feel certain and confident of our choices, when we know we are following our hearts, that is when our relationship with the universe, with nature, is in balance. When we are floundering, uncertain, or confused, we have lost our balance.

The fae of the *Mystic Faerie Tarot* believe that people with a strong connection to nature make balanced, healthy choices that consequently add to the health and balance of the universe. As guardians of the natural world, it furthers their cause to help us stay in proper relationship with ourselves, each other, and the world at large.

As you shuffle and lay out the cards, you may seem to wander at random through the faerie garden. But when using this deck, you can be assured that nothing is random; the faeries are guiding you toward your right path.

WHY TAROT?

Linda has created a superbly and intricately designed tool to help you find what you seek and so much more. Without further ado, let us visit the faerie garden and see what adventures await!

CHAPTER 2

The Major Arcana

You ARE ABOUT to enter the enchanted world of the mystic fae. This part of the garden is home to the Major Arcana. Here you will explore the larger secrets or mysteries of your life.

Some of the fae representing the archetypes are male, and some are female. This does not mean the cards specifically represent a man or a woman, though they can. Keep in mind these cards more accurately reflect masculine or feminine energy, and people express both types of energy in their lives.

0

THE FOOL

THE FOOL

THE QUINTESSENTIAL CHILD, this ragamuffin fae wears tattered clothes and an impish expression. He resides amidst white flowers that signify his innocence. Don't let the innocence mislead you, though; innocence does not denote a lack of wisdom. Traditionally, fools have been known to speak the truth when others are afraid to.

When we find ourselves in this part of the garden, we find answers that run beneath the wisdom of society, answers that may run contrary to what a grownup might ordinarily suggest. The choice shown may seem, well, foolish. Yet it is worth considering.

The Fool fae plays with bubbles, delicate orbs that may burst at the wrong touch. While he can toss them about with no fear of destroying them, for us humans, they represent a brief moment of wondrous choices. We are at a place where many things, maybe all things, are possible. The bubbles float lightly on the wind and may, at any moment, go off in an unexpected direction. That unpredictable tendency makes them a bit scary. Because these opportunities won't last long, we must have faith in our fancy, pick a path, and follow it with a happy heart.

The bells on his cap create a happy, playful sound whenever he moves. He can enjoy the enchanting notes without distraction. We, however, must be careful and remember that headpieces, hats, and caps are symbolic. Because they cover the head, they usually represent conscious thought. While he lives in his happy part of the garden where all possibilities exist, the bells are just part of the experience. For us, though, they are a warning to beware of overthinking. When we analyze too much, we may give in to fear and worry and thereby miss the magical opportunities that will disappear all too soon.

Your Message

In the Fool's garden, you are surrounded by enchanting choices that will vanish if you become distracted by analysis. This is not a time to make lists of pros and cons. Rather, it is a time to have childlike faith in the yearnings of your heart, and follow your dreams.

I

THE MAGICIAN

THE MAGICIAN

$\mathfrak{T}$HIS CONFIDENT FAE surrounds himself with a strange array of the magical and the mundane. On a ceremonial alter, he arranges a sword, a cup of water, and some pentacles, ancient and mystical symbols of the elements of the universe. He holds a wand, which is the fourth element. The playing cards also represent the four suits of the Minor Arcana, but in a more everyday appearance. They match up like this:

Wands = Clubs

Cups = Hearts

Swords = Spades

Pentacles = Diamonds

Whether a stage magician, charlatan, or a mythical wizard like Merlin, all magicians are tricky, and this fae is no exception. He understands the magical concept of "As above, so below." This means that things on a universal level are reflected on a mundane level. It also means that as you think, so you are. You create your experience with your thoughts. While the Fool is about not thinking, the Magician is all about thinking.

Our Magician fae knows how he wants things to be, and so he shuffles the cards, knowing they will turn out the way he wants. He has amazing talent and skill. This Magician, being fae, can shuffle and determine with confidence that what he creates will be in balance with the universe. For us humans, however, we must be careful. We must realize that while we have much power, we need to consider the consequences of our actions. The Magician fae knows this, and his clothing reflects it. He wears ordinary, mundane brown ... the raw material of life. On his shoulders, he wears a small cape of blue and red, representing thought and intent. This reminds him, and us, that the responsibility of our actions rests on our shoulders.

Your Message

While in this part of the garden, you are reminded that you have more control over your life than you may think or feel at the moment. That's a wonderful, empowering notion. But humans can be careless, thoughtless, or short-sighted. You must be aware that everything you do has consequences, sometimes further reaching or more dangerous than you can imagine. Like the Magician, you have power and ability; use it well.

II

THE PRIESTESS

A PICTURE OF perfect serenity, this shaman fae has connected herself on every level to what she values above all else. She chooses as her foundation a stone hewn from the ancient body of the earth itself, carved with spirals representing the cyclical nature of life. To direct her thoughts, she selects a headpiece that cradles the orb of the earth and contains feathers that symbolize birds, known for imparting secret knowledge to those who will listen.

Human shamans have been known to shape-shift into the forms of animals. The fae shaman instead connects to the natural world in a much deeper way—parts of her wings have become vines, connecting her to that which she loves best, the earth. She wears a green gown veined like a leaf, as if she would, if she could, become a plant herself, to be more connected to the earth. Hands are associated with manifestation, so she holds in her hands another earth orb as she would a great treasure.

She lives near a mighty oak. In both human and fae mythology, oak trees are associated with ancient universal power and symbolize a strong connection to the divine.

Your Message

When you find yourself in this part of the garden, your task is clear: you must identify what you value most in the world. The knowledge you seek exists in that value, regardless of any other circumstances. However that value finds expression—whether through a religious or spiritual belief system, through family, or through some other means—immerse yourself in it. Connect in every way possible. Create a sacred space like the Priestess has done, and stay there until you find perfect peace and serenity. In that space and in that moment, you will hear, if you are willing to listen, the answer you seek.

III

THE EMPRESS

IF WE MEET the Empress, we have wandered into probably the most lush and abundant part of the faerie garden. This fae is the archetypal mother, full of nurturing energy and a love for all things that delight the senses.

She sits atop a colorful poppy surrounded by lively and happy daisies. Everything in her garden is healthy, and diversity abounds. While it's true that she loves all growing things, she has a special place in her heart for the beginning of life, so it is natural that she herself is pregnant. And in spite of the vibrant colors and extraordinary shapes that surround her, she gazes on simple and plain-colored shafts of wheat. For here, in what may look like the end of life, is the beginning of life—the seeds of future wheat fields.

For all her physical sensuousness, she wears lavender, the color of spiritual wisdom. In order to nurture living things, she needs a higher knowledge. The wisdom she embodies seems simple in theory, but it is incredibly difficult, especially for humans, to practice. Notice her head is covered with tiny purple flowers and a few delicate feathers. She gives to all she nurtures enough wisdom for a strong beginning and enough beauty to sustain any trials. More than that she does not give, for she knows the difference between nurturing and controlling. She knows that things grow best when they grow true to their own natures.

Your Message

So you find yourself faced with a clear, if challenging, answer. You are in a position to nurture something. You must give enough of yourself to sustain life but not enough to smother the unique personality of the person, project, relationship, or situation you find entrusted to your care.

IV

THE EMPEROR

𝕿HOSE WHO HAPPEN upon the Emperor may think he is perhaps the most unhappy of all the fae. His garden is unlike most of the others, being sparser, and his stone throne is more ornately carved. Plus he's wearing shoes, which is definitely not faelike. We are correct in assuming that he volunteered to represent a uniquely human archetype that does not apply to the fae.

The role of Emperor carries much responsibility. This is evident immediately by the long, regal purple cloak trimmed in gold, showing that the welfare of many rests on his shoulders. He holds a shield bearing the likeness of a stylized eagle. Because it is a stylized eagle rather than a natural eagle, we know that he is charged with protecting and upholding a manmade legal or value system. The shoes, especially on a fae, represent social conventions.

He wears rams' horns because he leads and protects with a strong will. The oak leaves on his headpiece show that while he must uphold man-made institutions, he endeavors to incorporate timeless universal wisdom in all his decisions and actions. Indeed, we humans believe that our best legal, governmental, religious, social, and educational systems are based on some higher truth and serve a greater good by creating order so that all can live peaceful and fulfilling lives.

That is the key to creating and practicing human conventions. The fae would have us test our laws and beliefs to make sure they are in line with what is best not only for us but for the planet as a whole. We are responsible for our own well-being as well as that of the earth and all its inhabitants.

Your Message

When you are in the Emperor's garden, consider the institutions that may be behind your situation or question. Are they directing you in a way that is respectful of others and the future of the planet? Is there a way that you can change the institution so that it is more in line with universal balance? How can you choose to act that will benefit the greater good?

V

THE PRIEST

LIKE THE PRIESTESS, this fae is a shaman. Like her, he connects himself to the earth in the deepest way by wearing similar garb, sitting on an ancient stone throne and allowing his wings to vine into the earth itself.

The difference between these two shamans is significant. She closes her eyes, focuses inward, and listens quietly to the ancient wisdom of birds and tells us to look inward to find our truth and center. In this way, hers is a shamanism embodying a feminine energy.

The Priest, however, shows us a more masculine variation of shamanism. With his eyes open, he views his world through the eyes of his knowledge. He holds his orb with one hand while gesturing with the other, indicating a desire to manifest change in the world. His headpiece sports branches—rather than wisdom coming inward as with the Priestess, he roots himself in the earth, letting its wisdom branch outward.

The Priestess has an inner knowledge that we know as intuition, a way of knowing that we cannot always explain. The Priest is interested in formalizing ancient wisdom in a way that can be expressed and more easily shared with people. In human terms, he is both the sum of human knowledge and the way in which we pass that knowledge to future generations. In short, he is a teacher.

Your Message

When you are in the Priest's garden, be prepared to apply yourself and learn something. Your answer is to be found by dedicating yourself to a program of study of some sort. It may be furthering your formal education, deepening your spirituality, or learning a brand-new idea or practice. Whatever it is, it will require commitment and work on your part. The knowledge you seek is available to you, but you must find the right teacher ... or perhaps it is time for you to be a teacher for someone else.

VI

THE LOVERS

THE LOVERS

HESE PASSIONATE FAE are lost in each other's arms, where they find solace and a sense of completeness. They are an exquisite, beautiful union of feminine and masculine natures. Traditionally, feminine energy is based in the heart, and so the male fae lays his head gently on her heart. Masculine energy is said to reside in the mind, so the female fae embraces his head. Aware of their own weaknesses and the other's strengths, they willingly blend to complete a love in perfect balance.

This blissful pair resides amongst apple trees that magically bear both fruit and flower at the same time. By being together, they create an energy that provides continual nourishment—fruit for the moment and the promise of fruit in the future.

But this picture is not as simple as it first appears. Nor is it necessarily about love. It will, though, be about bringing magic and power into your life. Apples have long represented the need to make a choice. For example, although the Bible does not specify that the Tree of Knowledge of Good and Evil was an apple tree, it is generally depicted as an apple tree. When you wander into this part of the garden, you are probably faced with a choice. Which will it be, the fruit or the flower? Both may be desirable, but is one real magic and the other only glamour?

Your Message

The fae couple provides your clue: don't choose in haste, and don't necessarily choose what first catches your eye. Take your time. Assess your strengths and weaknesses. Imagine your life first with one choice and then the other. Which is best suited to provide balance in your life? Whatever you are considering bringing into your life, seek balance. Once you have chosen, hold on passionately, and magic and beauty will follow.

VII

THE CHARIOT

THROUGHOUT OUR WANDERINGS in the faerie garden, something in the sky may catch our attention. As we gaze upward, we might see a very self-assured fae driving an improbable yet lovely device drawn by two griffins.

The Charioteer fae illustrates a pretty amazing achievement. The black and white griffins represent opposite ideas, issues, or situations. Instead of being pulled willy-nilly in two different directions, this fae controls both, apparently without much effort. The griffins appear to struggle a bit, as if unaccustomed to such harnessing. She, however, stands tall and straight, unafraid and master of the Chariot.

Her headpiece shows her will that is shaped by her connection with the earth and with the wisdom of creatures of the air. Tiny orbs fall, as if from her headpiece. These orbs are a sort of faerie dust. They are magical in their effects—in this case, the ability to control magical beasts. This same magic is available to humans, as well, in the form of our will. When we rise above the chaos surrounding us, we can see the bigger picture and identify the main things that need our attention. Once we see our metaphorical griffins, we can confidently bring them under our control instead of feeling like a victim of circumstance.

Your Message

The Chariot fae reminds you to take a step back and make note of the major issues that are causing your situation. You will probably find there are two opposing forces pulling at you. This is a case of choosing both instead of one or another. The key is finding a way to convince both forces to go forward in the same direction. It may seem impossible, but if the Chariot crosses your path, you can know it is indeed possible and certainly to your benefit.

VIII

STRENGTH

STRENGTH

IN JOURNEYING THROUGH the faerie garden, we may wander into a thicket of trees and find an exquisitely captivating fae, Strength, and her dragon. Normally dragons are cause for alarm, but no need to worry in this case. Strength has things well in hand.

Dragons are ancient elementals and embody the great power and danger of the core of the earth itself. Yet from a distance, when they fly, they are elegant and graceful. As lovers of the earth, the fae are drawn to dragons, despite the peril—for not all of the fae can control dragons. The abilities of a dragon united with the wisdom of a fae make for a formidable force. Before a fae can unite with a dragon, she must understand it.

Because the fae are so deeply connected to the earth, for them, dragons represent their most raw, untamed selves, just like when humans talk of their "animal" side. So it isn't that difficult for a fae to understand a dragon; they simply need to examine their untamed motivations and impulses. This fae has done that and has found that not all base desires are bad. Rather, they are neutral sources of power to be channeled. So our Strength fae does not hide her admiration and connection to her dragon companion. Instead, she proudly adorns herself with symbols of the strength and power she has found through the relationship.

Your Message

If you have found yourself in this thicket as night is falling, and you're not quite sure what to do, Strength would remind you to understand your inner dragon. Reconnect with the part of you that is fiercely connected with the deep power of the earth. Find the molten center that will fire your courage. Then infuse it with wisdom so you can wield your power with elegance, grace, and precision.

IX

THE HERMIT

THE HERMIT

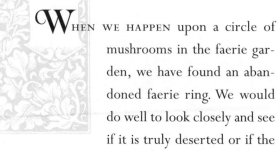

When we happen upon a circle of mushrooms in the faerie garden, we have found an abandoned faerie ring. We would do well to look closely and see if it is truly deserted or if the Hermit is there, lurking quietly in the shadows. Although a loner by nature, he does not entirely shun the company of his kind or even that of humans.

In spite of his rather cute appearance, this fae is on a serious quest: he seeks self-knowledge. His walking stick, which also serves as a wand, represents his will. His humble attire is decorated by two bright red buttons, signifying his desire to find what he seeks. The light he carries contains the knowledge he has acquired thus far. He sometimes uses the light to help others who may be on the same path find their way, as well.

He visits empty faerie rings because he can sense the energy that remains after his kind have left. He can examine, quiet and alone, the knowledge and wisdom that they have left behind. The Hermit prefers to do this on his own, so he can compare the collective social beliefs to those that reside in his own heart.

Although he is on a quest, it is different from most quests because he does not expect an end. This quest is a lifelong journey. With each step he takes and each experience he has, his understanding changes. Notice his ragged, loosely stitched cap. What he thinks and believes is constantly pieced together as time and new knowledge change what he thinks.

Your Message

The Hermit wants you to collect everything you think you know and spend some time alone with it. Compare it to the wisdom in your heart and to your current experiences. It is a challenge to hold on to what you believe while knowing that your understanding will constantly change. Release what doesn't work, keep what does, and continually re-create your own belief system.

X

WHEEL OF FORTUNE

WHEEL OF FORTUNE

W HEN WE WANDER into the presence
of the Wheel of Fortune, we
may be surprised by the pinkly
clad young faerie entrusted to
the protection of the wheel.
As she clamors and scampers
about, we think that she is playing with it more
than protecting it. Surely this incongruent image
holds a message for us.

The wheel itself is adorned with astrological symbols, denoting the turning of a solar year.
Faerie time runs different than our own, so we
should not interpret that too literally. Rather, it
shows the cycles of life, which may or may not
pass at the same speed all the time. Sometimes
phases of our lives move slowly, sometimes very
quickly. We humans often say life is a cycle with
ups and downs—by that we mean good times and
bad. However, this wheel doesn't show good and
bad, just different phases, each with their own
pluses and minuses.

The Wheel of Fortune isn't so much about what happens to us; these things are illustrated in the other cards of the tarot. It is more about our attitude toward the vicissitudes of life. Events that test us help us to learn and grow. Sometimes certain difficult events (like those represented by the Tower or Death) are necessary in order to bring better things to our lives (such as those represented by the Priestess or the Star).

And the happy, pink fae? She explores and values all experiences, seeking the gifts, the joys, and the lessons to be learned. If we are centered and committed to spiritual growth, we can share her childlike magic as we face our lives.

Your Message

Your answer isn't so much about what is happening to you now, but rather about how you face what is happening. See all challenges as opportunities. Look for spiritual lessons as you experience sadness. Remember to express gratitude through your joys. The more you learn to do this, the less traumatically you will be affected with each turning of the wheel.

XI

JUSTICE

THE FAE OF Justice lives in a mistletoe bush. While she looks very demure and gentle, she represents an incredibly powerful magic that is tied deeply to the core of the universe.

Her stone perch indicates her roots to the earth. However, she sits on a cushion decorated with spirals, indicating the cycles of life ... life as lived by people. The power she wields is a direct result of our individual actions. A human name for her power is karma, the justice of the universe. This is the most perfect and poetic of all justice systems. She holds the scales that weigh our actions and the sword that delivers our reward, whatever it may be. She is blindfolded, so she cannot help or hurt us. She can only mete out what we have earned.

Out of all the *Mystic Faerie* cards, this one speaks most clearly and succinctly the faerie's main message for us humans: what you do today directly creates what you will experience tomorrow. It is a message that we have heard many times, in many different ways. Our religious and spiritual systems express it, our legal system attempts to impose it, and even our everyday sayings remind us of it (you've made your bed, now you have to sleep in it).

Your Message

This fae wishes you to understand your power and your responsibility. If you are wondering why you are facing a situation, look to your past actions. If you can see how you brought yourself to this place, you can perhaps find a way to balance your karma. If you are facing a decision of how to behave in a situation, consider the future ramifications. Choose your actions wisely, and carefully make a bed you will be happy to sleep in.

XII

THE HANGED FAE

WALKING AMIDST THE lovely white flowers we may hear a quiet giggle. As we follow the sounds we'll see a young fae gently swinging from the vines.

The bubbles are reminiscent of the Fool fae. And there are many similarities between the two, although the differences are significant. Both these fae are about following a path that may not be condoned by others. The fear for us humans with following the bubbles we find in the Fool's garden is that of not knowing where they will lead.

After we have found our courage and followed the bubbles, we will often face the challenge of the Hanged Fae's garden. We will have to take a stand based on our choice. Again, we will probably run the risk of incurring the disapproval of others. That is the sacrifice of standing firm in our beliefs.

If this fae is all about standing firm, why is he hanging by a thread upside down? It is one thing

THE HANGED FAE

to follow our hearts. But when we have to take a decisive action, we may be turning our world upside down. We may risk losing things we value by taking the stand—for example, the approval of friends or security.

Notice the Hanged Fae's attitude, though. He is relaxed and confident that his beliefs, represented by the vines, will not fail him. He giggles quietly, as if at a secret delight. He knows he may look silly, but at this moment, there is nowhere else he'd rather be.

Your Message

In the Hanged Fae's garden, your answer is that of sacrifice and faith. You will be called on to sacrifice something for that which you hold dear. You should have the faith of your convictions and know that all will turn out well in the end. Although it may be scary at first, once you actually do it, you will experience a relaxed happiness and a knowledge that you've done exactly what you should.

XIII

DEATH

AVEN-HAIRED AND RAVEN-WINGED, the pale fae of the Underworld rests on a human skull, both inviting and daring us to enter her realm. Like the Hermit, she resides amidst mushrooms, the markers of faerie rings long past, honoring the memories of those who have already passed. Although she appears in the prime of her faerie life, the horns on her shoulders speak of her dragon ancestry, ancient and elemental.

Her beguiling beauty results from her deep knowledge of the secrets of death. For humans, death is frightening because we know neither it nor what lies beyond it. So we are both attracted and repelled by her. While she does hold the knowledge of the experience of physical death, she cannot share this with us entirely. It is not meant for us to know. And she reigns over all deaths, not just that of the physical realm.

Although we only experience one physical death in this life, we experience thousands of other sorts of deaths during our life. Life, as we know, is a cycle, and death is part of that cycle. Phases of our life end, others begin. Relationships bloom, flourish, and sometimes die. What we believe changes and passes away as we grow spiritually. And we know that where there is death, there is birth; where there is darkness, there is also light.

Our experiences have shown us that regardless of the light following darkness, the darkness is still hard to live through. And so this is no merely pretty faerie promising us eternally happy times. She does not diminish the pain of death in all its forms. Instead, she reminds us that growth, including spiritual growth, comes at great cost. To face it, to move through it, and to experience the birth of new life requires courage and strength.

Your Message

The answer you find in the garden of the fae of Death is that of acceptance and hope. It is time to accept the passing of something from your life. Pain, sadness, and a sense of loss are part of the experience. Find strength and hope from the knowledge that something else will arrive in your life to ease the pain and sadness and fill the empty space.

XIV

TEMPERANCE

TEMPERANCE

WANDERING INTO A birch grove, we find a sight of quietly exuberant beauty. Although an apparent contradiction, that is the essence of the Temperance fae. She is kin to the Charioteer fae but more mature and experienced. Notice that her headpiece is small and simple, for her power is not so much that of the will of the mind as of wholly being. Like the birch trees that surround her, she gracefully bends with the winds of fate but does not break under the pressure.

She sits solidly on a stone carved with a single fluid spiral. She sees life and her role in it as a long, single, elegant dance. She endlessly pours water from a jar to a bowl. Her elegant flow of life is seamless and constant. No matter what the circumstance, she always is exactly what she is. To be always who she is requires not rigidity but fluidity. Without thinking, she imperceptibly adjusts her energy to maintain perfect balance within any situation.

TEMPERANCE

Her vibrant yellow gown and wings express her strong, glowing inner strength that arises from such certain confidence. She faces all that comes her way with expectant surety, knowing that she can handle anything with the utmost grace and beauty. Unlike the Charioteer, who controls opposing forces with the power of her will, Temperance blends them into a perfect and flawless balance within her very being.

Your Message

While it may be impossible for humans to maintain this state of being indefinitely, Temperance's answer to you is to mind your reactions. Let whatever you do, think, or feel be appropriate and beneficial to whatever you are facing. Don't add to the chaos or drama by overreacting. Your task now is to center yourself and do whatever is necessary to establish balance in the situation.

XV

THE DEVIL

THE DEVIL

EVELING IN HIS horns, cloven feet, tail, and fiery red wings, the Devil fae frolics in a part of the garden that is dangerous for humans. He resembles, even more closely than the Death fae, his dragon ancestry, for he does represent the most basic of drives and desires. His earring and beaded beard show that he has adorned and altered these fundamental energies. He recognizes them, celebrates them, and controls them. As a fae, he is connected to the earth and therefore in balance with it—but just barely. It is his nature that he dances on the edge, balancing and playing with boundaries.

Humans are so far removed from our fundamental ancestry that we often don't know how to express that part of ourselves, either in society or in our lives. Consequently, we often deny these desires. Because of this repression, our instinctual and sensual drives often show up in ways that are not necessarily good for us, others, or the universe.

Another way that this disconnect from our basic nature plays out is when a certain desire will not only demand satisfaction but begin to control a person. This leads to addictions, obsessions, and other unhealthy patterns.

Your Message

If you are in the Devil's garden, your answers will not be easy, but they will be freeing. At some level, something is controlling you, and thus you are not in control of your life. Identify what it is that holds you in bondage. Only then can you free yourself. And finally, our impish fae would tell you to not be afraid of all your desires. Enjoy the ones you can in ways that are beneficial to you and others, and don't give the destructive ones any foothold in your life.

XVI

THE TOWER

HE FAE ARE long-lived creatures. They love nature and all things beautiful. They are talented and skilled craftspeople. If they choose to live in a dwelling, they will create for themselves something of graceful lines following the design of nature while expressing their belief in the interconnectedness of all life. Because of their long lives, they can see and accept the bigger picture, including the ultimate destruction of wondrous things—whether a forest or a work of art. Nature purifies itself out of necessity. It maintains its own balance. And so if a tree, garden, or fae dwelling is destroyed by nature, the fae know it is for the greater good.

For us to happen upon the destruction of such a lovely creation is heartbreaking. We see all the cunning little carvings and are awed by such a perfect union of nature and craftsmanship. The mushrooms, marking out the faerie rings, remind us of the happy social gatherings enjoyed in this place. It was a pleasant site that served its purpose very well. And we, because of our short lives, have a difficult time understanding why a perfectly good dwelling should be leveled.

People use tarot cards similarly to how they use dreams. We interpret symbols to find meaning applicable to our lives. In dreams, houses often represent the self. That is why this image, the Tower, is hard for us. On a deeper level, it means the destruction of what defines ourselves. Each of us crafts a worldview or belief system that helps us navigate our world. And then sometimes something comes along and—*bam*—a perfectly good worldview is destroyed.

Your Message

If you see the burning of a fae tower, you know that some belief that you hold dear, that is a deep part of how you define yourself, is being called into question. You are experiencing something that doesn't mesh with it, something that will cause it to tumble down. It will no longer be true for you. Whatever it is, its destruction is necessary to create a new image of yourself that will serve you better.

XVII

THE STAR

ANDERING AMONG THE remains of a
once-glorious forest, we can
hear the gentle flow of water,
the slight movement of water
in a pool, and we think we
almost hear the twinkling of
starlight playing on the water's surface. As we follow the sounds, we happen on this quiet picture
of cool serenity and restful peace.

A fae as pale as starlight lounges comfortably
on some distinctly uncomfortable-looking rocks
at the water's edge; it's as if she herself is flowing,
like water, over the rocks. She is clad in the soft-
est of blues, a gown that curves over her like the
water running over the earth. Her delicate wings
sparkle under the stars.

The Star is not like a real star; she does not
burn, she is not fiery. She is water in its most
healing aspects. She refreshes and renews; she
gives hope. But like a star, she does guide us. The
depths of her power are endless, like the eter-
nal streams of water she pours into the pool and

onto the earth. One foot is in the water, showing her connection to the subconscious. The other
is on the ground, for her concern is also for the
conscious. To those weary in body and soul, she
promises peace.

Your Message

Your answer, should you find yourself by the
Star's pool, should be very welcome. Whatever
has been trying your spirit, whatever difficulties
you've been facing, whatever sadness has torn
your heart, the Star brings a time of serene quiet; a safe, cool place where you can be refreshed
and find hope. Once you are renewed and feeling stronger, she will serve as your guiding star to
help you find your way. But first, rest.

XVIII

THE MOON

THE MOON

IN THE DARKNESS and in the shadows, everything looks different ... invisible or larger than life, muted or oddly bright. The Moon fae's illumination is enchanting and beguiling, for those who keep their wits about them. It can be deceptive and dangerous for those who are less careful. Surrounded by daisies, she appears as simple and clear as sunlight. But with the Moon fae, all is not as it seems. While she can seem either troublesome or charming, she is really neither or both—her effect is based entirely on our perception of her.

Her wolf companion shows how our animal nature is attracted to and stirred up by her presence. In fact, just as wolves are compelled to react to the moon in the night sky, so too does a part of the human psyche. We act more intuitively, we dream more vividly, we feel more deeply.

She sits on a stone carved with a crayfish, an unlikely symbol for a Moon fae. But remember, things are not as they seem. A crayfish has long represented a creature that has crawled out of the water—our subconscious—and it is something that we fear.

In the magical light of the Moon, wild wolves and monstrous crayfish can appear beautiful, and simple daisies can seem threatening. And that is the danger—not seeing what really is. The Moon fae gives neither dreams nor nightmares. She lights the world, and we see whatever we choose to see.

Your Message

If you are lost in the Moon fae's night, your answer is as shadowy as moonlight itself. What is clear is that your subconscious is stirred up. What is emerging—your fears, your hopes, or your dreams? Pay attention to your intuition and your dreams. Listen carefully for messages from the universe. Take care, and make sure you want to seek the truth. In this situation, you are in danger of seeing what you want to see or hearing what you want to hear.

XIX

THE SUN

THE SUN

IF WE TRAVEL to the Sun fae's garden, we will, first of all, be momentarily blinded by the most vivid splash of orange. The fae and the nearby sunflowers are covred in an orange so vibrant, it is almost laughing with joy. Unlike the Moon, this card is quite simple, and things are pretty much what they seem.

The Sun fae and her child are enjoying a glorious moment of pure and blissful joy. There is no reason, no circumstance—just a happiness so strong that it colors everything around it, surrounding the moment in a luminous glow.

This type of joy results from a feeling of connection and ease with the universe, which is probably pretty common for faerie folk. For us humans, it's a fairly extraordinary experience.

THE SUN

Your Message

The answer you find here in the Sun fae's garden is a happy one. You can expect a time of happiness, joyous optimism, and wondrous energy. This is a real gift. Enjoy it!

XX

JUDGEMENT

JUDGEMENT

WHEN WE WALK among the lilies, we see a luminous glow and hear, very quietly at first, the sound of a trumpet. It grows louder. As we search for its source, our eyes slowly focus on an image so light, so pale, that we hardly believe it exists. This delicate fae, with her gentle white gown and powerful wings, bears a heavy title, for she is the fae of Judgement.

Her message is not for everyone. There are those who neither see nor hear her. Lilies are often associated with death, and it usually requires a death of some sort for anyone, especially non-fae folk, to hear and see her. Something in our lives has or will or should pass because we are being called to something new.

For those who can see her, she shimmers and glows with truth and natural beauty. Even more amazing is the sound of her trumpet. Its message is essentially the same for everyone, but different, too. It calls those who hear to a higher level of being, to do something different, to serve the universe and those in it in a new way.

The strong wings of Judgement are no fluke. They are symbols, reminders, that for those who heed her call, they shall be lifted up to a higher spiritual level than they have yet known.

Your Message

When you meet the fae of Judgement, it is time to look carefully at your life and the possibilities before you. There is something you should be doing, something that would be a significant change from what you are doing. Whatever this something is, it is for the benefit of the universe and essential to your spiritual growth. To hear your guidance clearly, open your heart and mind and be willing to accept the message.

XXI

THE WORLD

NESTLED IN A rose garden, we find a symbolic scene. The fae are the keepers of the garden and value perfect balance in the universe. For the fae we have met in this garden, Earth is what they value above all else. They cherish Earth and show it with a crown to indicate that its needs reign over their decisions and actions.

These particular faeries wear laurel crowns that intertwine around Earth. They consider it their greatest and most worthy achievement when Earth is in perfect balance. When Earth is well tended, that's how they know they've lived up to their highest potential.

When we see the World fae, we humans are reminded that we have many ways to fulfill our best potential. Throughout our lives, we experience various achievements that give us satisfaction and pride. Sometimes they are little, everyday things, like helping someone with a task that is troubling her. Sometimes they are larger, milestone-like events, like completing an educational program or participating in a charitable organization. Whatever they are, we should always remember to enjoy the sense of achievement that results from a job well done.

Your Message

If you find yourself in the rose garden, you may have either recently completed or soon will complete an important task. You are ready to enjoy success and receive the happy congratulations of others. These moments are, unfortunately, too infrequent and are always the results of some effort on your part, so do not sweep past it in your hurry to look for your project. If you haven't recently completed something, the desire for this feeling is directing you to find a challenge. Listen to your heart, for you are clearly ready to take on something exciting.

CHAPTER 3

The Minor Arcana

THE CARDS OF the Minor Arcana illustrate the joys and the beauty as well as the trials and the tribulations of everyday life. Throughout human history, people have used stories, myths, and legends to make sense of life and learn lessons in order to live better lives. The *Mystic Faerie Tarot* honors that rich and creative history by telling a story with each suit—new faerie tales that will help you more easily understand the meaning of the cards.

The Wands tell a tale of enterprise and adventure as two faeries go off to seek their fortune. Their story shows the triumphs and dangers possible when undertaking any project. In the cards, the Wands are represented by actual wands.

The Cups weave a tragic yet ultimately inspiring tapestry of love. We follow the heights and depths throughout the years of an unlikely match in the faerie world. The Cups are the magical celandine blooms.

The Swords touchingly illustrate the despair and the resourcefulness of two young fae as they face a distressing fate and their queen's valiant efforts to save her people. The Swords are represented by the thorns on the roses.

The Pentacles show us the uplifting experience of an industrious faerie whose hard work and planning takes an unexpected turn, and how taking advantage of a lucky opportunity works to the benefit of all involved. The Pentacles show up in these cards as pentacles.

These charming tales serve two purposes. First, each story contains a moral for us from the faerie world. These morals are special messages that the faeries would like all humans to know. They believe that if we apply these morals to our lives in general, we will deepen our connection with each other and the earth. Secondly, when using these cards in a reading about your life, each card also has a message that applies to the question asked.

WANDS

THE
GRAND
ADVENTURE

ACE

ONCE UPON A time, on a warm summer evening, a faerie clan gathered to hear stories told by their elders. The stories were about faraway places and strange sights. After the elders went off to sleep, some of the younger fae decided they wanted to travel and seek new things so they'd have their own stories to tell. The idea of going off and having adventures delighted them, and they danced with glee to celebrate their decision.

To bring luck to their enterprise, they crafted a wand, representing their strength and resolve, from an oak branch. They topped it with a red crystal that appeared to hold a fiery energy within its core, which, they said, showed their focus, determination, and passion. Finally, they wound two griffin feathers around the crystal to bring wisdom and fortune to their endeavor. After it was finished, they put it in the middle of the faerie ring that their dancing had created. When they returned, they would sit in this very spot surrounded by their clan and tell grand stories of their adventures. And so it was.

Years later, the faeries came to call this spot the Place of Beginnings. Whenever any fae wanted to start a new venture, they'd sit in the Place of Beginnings and make their plans.

Your Message

You have the need to begin something new. Make a space, either physical or in your mind, to consider a plan. Take an inventory. Do you have the strength, resolve, focus, determination, and passion necessary? Do you have access to the wisdom and resources necessary? Do you have a clear picture of your goal?

2

ONE DAY, YEARS and years after the Place of Beginnings was created, two young faeries decided they wanted to go seek their fortune together. Sitting near the wand, they were inspired and formed a partnership, shaking hands and agreeing to stick together through thick and thin. They were very enthusiastic, filled with dreams and desires. They talked of possibilities, and although they weren't sure what they wanted, they were certain that they'd find nothing but good fortune and fabulous adventures.

Your Message

A partnership is available to you. It is likely that the possibilities of this partnership are exciting and inspiring. However, it is also likely that there is much that is still unknown about the partner or the nature of the partnership. Events depicted by the Wands cards include an element of swiftness ... they enter and exit your life quickly. You will need to decide: are you willing to make this commitment, or will you let the opportunity pass by?

3

T HE TWO FRIENDS realize that although they don't know what they want to achieve, they do know that they cannot set off without a plan. They look through a book of maps created by other fae who went on adventures before them. The maps have descriptions of the things that could be found in each location. The two friends, having heard great tales of the wondrous phoenix, decide that they want to explore the land of the fire sprites to see this great creature for themselves. They dream that the phoenix grants them a feather filled with powerful magical properties. That would certainly make their fortune. And so they finally have a plan and a goal.

Your Message

It is almost time to move forward. But first, you must consider the possibilities. Do some research, write out all the options, and think about what goal is most appealing to you. Make a map of your journey and a list of the things you'll need. You'll want to be sure that you'll have everything you'll need along the way, that you know where you want to go, and that you'll know what you want to do once you've arrived.

4

HE TWO ADVENTUROUS friends are having a pretty easy time. The fae who have gone this way before left faerie-ring markers along the route. While they've enjoyed the travel, they are ready for something exciting to happen, and as they approach the very edges of the fire sprites' dwellings, they meet a lovely young sprite. She is carrying an egg with golden speckles that she found. She likes the two energetic faeries and decides to give them the egg, hoping it will bring them luck. Even though they aren't sure what it contains, they are sure it's valuable, so they accept it and thank her.

Your Message

An unexpected gift finds its way into your life. Someone wishes you well and wants to help you along your path. You may not know exactly how to incorporate the gift, but it is valuable and you should handle it carefully. Accept the gift graciously, with joy and gratitude.

5

AFTER THE GENEROUS sprite goes along her way, the two friends stay to discuss this unexpected turn of events. They know that the sprite wished them well, but she didn't know what the egg contained. They debate about what to do with the egg. One thinks that it is a dragon egg and that they should leave it behind and move on. The other thinks that it is a phoenix egg and that they should stay and tend it until it hatches. This is their first disagreement, and it is making them both feel unsettled. In the end, they agree to stay and at least see what is in the egg. If it is a dragon, they agree to leave it.

Your Message

You face a time of debate or even argument, perhaps with another person or people (or perhaps within yourself). An agreement must be reached. To reach an agreement, make sure you both get to express your reasons, and make every attempt to listen carefully to each other (or carefully examine all sides of the conflict within yourself). If neither of you are convinced of the other's point of view, work together to form a compromise.

WANDS

6

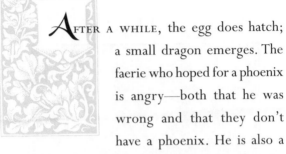

AFTER A WHILE, the egg does hatch; a small dragon emerges. The faerie who hoped for a phoenix is angry—both that he was wrong and that they don't have a phoenix. He is also a little frightened of the dragon. The other friend is happy that he was right. He is so consumed with his victory over guessing correctly that he decides that having a dragon is a good thing. He holds the dragon high as if he'd won a trophy while his thwarted friend watches, his anger, disappointment, and fear growing.

Your Message

You have achieved something, whether it is something you worked hard toward or something that was as easy as a guess. You feel good about the achievement. You want to celebrate and be recognized for what you have done. If you have truly achieved something you have worked toward, enjoy your sense of victory and celebrate with those who care about you. However,

6 OF WANDS

if you've won a questionable victory, beware of a false sense of achievement, and be aware of the feelings of those who matter more to you than the victory itself.

7

T̲HE̲ ̲T̲W̲O̲ ̲F̲R̲I̲E̲N̲D̲S̲, who agreed to stick together through good and bad, are facing very bad times, indeed. The dragon is growing at an incredibly fast rate. And although they originally agreed to leave the dragon behind, one friend cannot bring himself to do so. He thinks they can raise it and tame it, controlling it for their own purposes. The other friend doesn't think that a dragon can be tamed, that it will be nothing but trouble and should be released to live as dragons live and not be brought into the lives of their family and friends. They argue heatedly, and there is no sign of any middle ground. The partnership is threatened.

Your Message

There is a difference of opinion and no sense of compromise. You want something that your partner does not. Neither of you can see the other's point of view. Unless one of you backs down, the only resolution is to end the partnership and

break your agreement with each other. Sometimes this happens. Make sure what you want is
worth the cost. If it is, then stand up for yourself,
no matter how difficult. If not, then swallow your
pride and give in or find a compromise.

WANDS

8

8 OF WANDS

THINGS HAPPEN VERY quickly after the fight. The friend who wants to leave the dragon threatens to destroy it because he thinks it is the only way to release its hold over his friend. The other friend doesn't want to leave the dragon and also doesn't want it destroyed. Feeling like he has no choice or any time to think about his decision, he climbs on the dragon's back, and they fly away together. With this act, decided in a heated and rushed moment, he severs the friendship and chooses his future.

Your Message

The message of this card is very simple: events are moving very quickly. You are compelled to act, almost without thinking. You must go along with your gut feeling and trust that it is the right choice.

9

9 OF WANDS

$\mathcal{T}$HE FAERIE IS now alone with his dragon. The dragon has grown so huge that he doesn't know how he will control it. In the morning, he sees blood on the dragon's lips. He doesn't know where it has been or what it has done. Although he is on the outskirts of a village, it is a close enough journey for a dragon. Fae and sprite lives are at risk. When he started out on this journey, he never expected it to end like this. He realizes that it was the choices he made that brought him here. The faerie accepts his responsibility and considers what to do next.

Your Message

You have made choices that have consequences. The consequences may be ones you like or ones you don't like. The outcomes may be exactly what you intended or not what you had in mind at all. Nevertheless, they are the results of your actions. You have to accept them and decide how to live with them.

WANDS

10

HE FAERIE AND his dragon live far from any other fair folk. But still, a dragon can fly far very easily. The faerie spends his time keeping the dragon bound and caring for it as best he can. He believes that it is his burden to carry, that he must take care of the dragon while keeping it away from villages. It is a heavy burden and doesn't make him or the dragon happy. It is a sad story. But one has to wonder: why doesn't the faerie let the dragon fly away to join the other dragons who live far away from faeries, pixies, sprites, and elves?

Your Message

You are carrying a very heavy burden. Responsibilities overwhelm you. Your life feels pretty miserable. There will be times in your life when this is true. In those cases, you must find hope and strength where you can, such as turning to other people for help or inspiration. However, you should make sure that you aren't carrying a burden needlessly. When you are feeling over-whelmed, examine your load. Do you really need to be responsible for it all? Is there perhaps a better way to handle the load? Is there some way to make your path easier?

WANDS

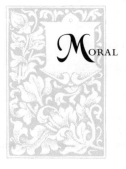

MORAL

You always have to face the consequences of your actions, but do not let consequences become your fate. It is never too late to make better choices.

CUPS

THE
MAGIC
CEL'ANDINE

ACE

ACE OF CUPS

ONCE UPON A time, in a strange part of the faerie world betwixt the land and the water, there was a place that was neither land nor water. In this unlikely and uninhabited space, there grew a celandine on a lily pad. Since few fae passed this place, few knew it was there. Fewer still stopped to investigate. Years went by, and the few passers-by began noticing a tiny yet beautiful chalice that seemed to grow from this celandine. If any stayed around long enough, they'd notice it produced odd bubblelike pearls. Or pearl-like bubbles. No one knew for sure which.

More time passed, and tales of this celandine grew into legend. It was said to be a magical place, between the land and the water, where the seeds of true love grew from a strange cuplike flower. It was further said that if two fae passed through that area together and shared a seed of true love, they would be given a great gift. True love would bind them together forever. But such

ACE OF CUPS

a gift came with a price—the two would have to successfully overcome many hardships or be fated to a lifetime of great loneliness, separated forever by their failure to nurture the gift of true love. Because more celandines kept growing in the area, the fae said that each time a pearl was shared, a new flower grew.

Even the most adventurous faeries explored this land by themselves. While the promise of true love was bewitching, the consequence of being found unworthy was one they were not willing to risk.

Your Message

You are faced with the opportunity to pursue a new relationship. Don't let the fear of what might happen get in your way. Approach it with the intention of making it the best it can be, and if it is a good thing, don't neglect it—continue to nurture and strengthen it.

CUPS

2

ONE DAY A young, beautiful, and adventurous water nymph heard of the magical celandine with its promise of true love and went in search of it. Likewise, an equally young, handsome, and adventurous young wood elf did the same. They discovered each other, the magic celandine, and a bubblelike pearl at the same time. Although they were from different races, she accepted the pearl when the elf offered it. Convinced of the legend's truth and promise, they pledged their love and commitment to each other.

Your Message

You are at the beginning of an exciting partnership, romantic or otherwise. Everything feels magical and wonderful. Enjoy this time to the utmost, and store up the memories of it. The happiness of this period will give you strength through the harder times. You are finding it easy to make promises and vows right now. These memories will help you keep the promises later, when you may wonder why you ever made them.

3

AFTER FROLICKING, EXPLORING, and laughing the day away with her new friend, the nymph went home. She gathered her friends to hear her tale, celebrate her great luck, and admire her pearl. They swam and danced and giggled, as young girls do at the thought of romance. None of them had ever known an elf; they'd only heard stories. Her friends joked about the nymph loving an elf and made fun of the strange ways of the woodland dwellers. The nymph tried to ignore the jokes, but they hid in the back of her mind.

Your Message

Celebrate the great things in your life with the great friends of your life. Let your hair down, kick up your heels, and dance just for the joy of it. Your friends help increase your joy and support you in times of sorrow. They are a wonderful blessing. Just remember that while they are an important part of your life, they are not your life. Don't let their opinions affect your choices. Good friends will always celebrate your joy, no matter what.

CUPS

4

HE NYMPH AND the elf met often in the celandine garden. They learned about each other and at first found their differences delightful and exciting. After a while, though, they tired of talking about themselves. They began to focus on their differences, which eventually became annoyances. They wondered if there was enough commonality to hold the friendship together. The confused little nymph kept thinking about her friends and wondering if their jokes held more truth than she wanted to admit. Eventually the nymph and the elf stopped visiting the celandine garden.

Your Message

There are no two ways about it—you are bored and annoyed. Whether it is your partner (romantic or business), family member, or friend, you have had it with the relationship. It's going nowhere and has nothing to offer—or so you think. Before writing it off, think about what you've put into the relationship and how you'd really feel if it was over. If it's done, it's done. If not, do your part to revitalize it. You'll both be happier in the long run.

5

EVERY ONCE IN a while, the little nymph found herself missing her elf and wondering what he was doing. She would see or do something that she wished she could tell him about, feeling a sharp pain that went deeper each time it happened. The crying spells became more and more frequent. She began to regret that she let her friends' words stay in her mind. She wished she had worked harder at the friendship. She no longer found comfort in her friends, becoming increasingly lonely and making her home far from her kin at the edge of the celandine garden.

Your Message

A relationship with someone you cared for has ended. The pain of it isn't getting any easier to bear. Instead, it seems to be getting worse. While mourning a loss is normal and necessary, be careful. If you mourn too long—if you isolate yourself from others in your life—you are creating a dangerous situation. Find someone to help you through this difficult time.

CUPS

6

THE LITTLE WATER nymph's loneliness became greater, isolating her from her friends and all happiness. There was only one thing that brought her any relief from her sorrow. She spent days on end gazing into the pearl her elf gave her those long years ago in the celandine garden. When she looked into it, she relived all their happy times. At first, she was surprised at how many beautiful memories they created together. She started to imagine all the wonderful memories as yet unmade and all the things she'd like to experience with him if she only could.

Your Message

Something or someone is missing from your life, and you feel that loss quite deeply. You find a sort of peace in living in the past. Memories are funny things and easily altered by time and distance. They can be bewitching and invasive. They can even be tyrants. Reliving memories can be comforting, but don't let them keep you from living in the present.

CUPS

7

AFTER ONE OF her infrequent outings with her friends, which she found wholly unsatisfying, the lonely and unhappy nymph went home. As usual, she looked at her pearl. It was blank; she saw nothing. She remembered the legend and wondered if her memories would be taken from her, leaving her with only a great emptiness. She realized that she was at a crossroads, and a choice was before her that would decide her fate forever. She could embrace the nothingness, or she could admit her mistake and find her dear wood elf. He may not want her, but she could at least try.

Your Message

You are faced with choices—maybe two, maybe more. Maybe you're feeling unsettled and confused. You may not be quite sure what to believe. You're certainly not absolutely sure what to decide. The time has come, though, for you to examine the choices thoroughly, and pick one. Somewhere deep inside you, you do know what you want. Focus on your heart, and make a decision.

8

THE WATER NYMPH, while glad to have made a decision, is not quite sure how to find the wood elf. She has never been in the woods; she doesn't know how to survive there. She has no idea how vast "the woods" might be. She has absolutely no way to know how to find him. As she wanders around the celandine garden, searching for inspiration or even a tiny idea, she meets and befriends a dragonfly who knows where several elfish villages are. After hearing the nymph's tragic tale, the dragonfly agrees to help her find her beloved elf.

Your Message

You searched your soul; you feel like you're living a lukewarm life. You now know what you want to do. All that is left is to make the necessary arrangements and do it. It probably won't be easy. You'll need to be brave and strong; you will be. There's not much choice, really, because if you don't do this thing, you will always wonder "what if." Now is the time to seek your destiny.

9

AFTER SOME EXTRAORDINARY and dangerous adventures with the dragonfly, the water nymph finally finds her wood elf. He has been as sad and lonely as she. Both of them had been longing, dreaming, and wishing. As they joyfully embrace, they feel like all their wishes have been fulfilled, and all the years of pain are swept away in one sweet moment. Their devotion and commitment is rekindled, tempered with the wisdom of time and experience. They both feel lucky that they learned their lessons before it was too late.

Your Message

This card is traditionally known as the Wish Card. Your dearest wish coming true—it's a moment we'd all love to experience. It's not often, though, that wishes are simply granted. You can, however, help them along by figuring out what needs to happen to make them come true. You probably have more power to realize your dream than you even know. Make your wishes come true.

10

YEARS LATER, THEY are still together, living a life neither in the water nor on the land, neither entirely nymph nor entirely elf, but a life totally unique to themselves. They spend their days together, happy and grateful. They treasure their pearl, the symbol of their love—the love that brought them together in the first place and gave them a second chance. They've discovered that they have no problem finding things to do together. And when they run out of things to talk about, they are content enough just being in each other's presence.

Your Message

This card shows perfect peace, contentment, and happiness. Do you have it? Be grateful and treasure it every day. Do you want it? It is usually the reward for years of hard work and careful attention to the details of a relationship. It hardly ever just happens. Truth be told, it's a lot of work. And it's totally worth it.

MORAL

Sometimes love takes time, but mostly it takes effort. Always seek understanding and reconciliation.

SWORDS

THE BLUE
ROSE

ACE

Once upon a time, in a time so long ago that even the long-lived faeries don't remember, there grew a single blue rose. It lived in the midst of the fae's ancestors' garden home. It was a spectacular plant, which they believed had strong magical power. When the rose was vibrant and healthy, so too were they. When it was wilted and stressed, their village was likewise. Then a well-intentioned faerie king decided that he did not want the well-being of his people dependent on something so variable as the health of a delicate plant.

He ordered the most skilled artisans and the most knowledgeable magicians to craft a sword to hold the power of the blue rose. At the height of the rose's vibrancy, they harvested a large thorn from the plant. From it, they fashioned a glorious sword embellished with their most sacred symbols. After it was finished, they laid it near the rose and used their best magic to draw power from the rose into the sword. When they were done, they attempted to pick it up to deliver it to their king, but discovered no one could touch it.

They had no choice but to leave it where it lay. They wondered what went wrong. Eventually, they realized the folly of trying to alter the natural order of life and eliminate trials from their experiences. In their embarrassment, they ignored the sword, letting the garden overgrow around it and hide it from their sight.

Your Message

You are facing a challenge or problem of some sort. Instead of bemoaning the fact that life has ups and downs, learn to find healthy ways to face the challenge or solve the problems, or develop realistic ways to cope with them.

2

As the generations came and went, the sword was forgotten. As time passed, more and more blue rose plants grew until the entire garden was filled with them. It came to be that the reigning faerie queen appointed two favored companions to care for the blue roses in the garden. One day, the two gentle rose tenders noticed a bud that stood out from the rest. It had a unique glow and energy; clearly it was a magic rose. They vowed to protect and cosset the little rosebud, spending hours tending it and filling it with their love. When it bloomed, they would show their queen this great gift. Until then, it would be their secret.

Your Message

You face a choice. You are in a situation or relationship or involved in a project that is requiring too much of your time and energy. Your life may become unbalanced as you neglect other responsibilities. Any situation that compels you

to keep secrets from those you love is dangerous and unhealthy. Be honest with yourself about
what you are doing and why. Making the right
choice now could eliminate bigger problems or
even tragedy later.

3

HEY RETURNED ONE day to find their beloved rose dying. Their hearts were broken. More than broken ... it felt as if their hearts were being ripped from their bodies. The pain and shock was so powerful, the ground around them became cluttered with the crystal tears they cried. They could not believe that all of their love did not protect the rose at all. Their great plans of presenting the magic rose to their queen were for naught. All they feel is their loss, and they mourn that loss unceasingly for days.

Your Message

When something you have loved or have invested in is lost, it hurts. If you've lost something, don't try to act like it doesn't matter. Acknowledge your pain, and let it express itself. You may be afraid that if you allow those feelings out, they will engulf you and overtake your life. It may feel like that for a while, but eventually your mourning will be over, and you'll be able to start healing.

SWORDS

4

*E*VENTUALLY, WORN OUT with grief, they could cry no longer. Nor could they face the tragic situation, for they had no strength left. They fell asleep under the dying rosebud, comforting each other and hoping that when they woke up they would find it had been nothing but a bad dream, and their rose would be fine. Their sleep is deep, long, and undisturbed by dreams. The rose weeps while they slumber, the last of its strength slowly flowing into the earth. The dire reality of the dying rose hovers above them, the horrible situation unchanged despite their mourning.

Your Message

If you are facing a difficult situation and find that you don't have the strength to deal with it, then don't. Take a break, and get some rest. Your mind cannot function well if you're worn out. Even though your problem will still be there when you wake up or come back to it, you will be much better equipped to deal with it wisely. And sometimes people do find solutions to problems in their dreams.

5

AFTER MANY HOURS, the garden tenders wake up. They find that not only is the rosebud still dying, but now things are going from bad to worse: the whole garden is dying around them. Luckily, they are refreshed from their long sleep and decide to find a solution to their problem. They discuss and debate, trying to determine what is to blame for this catastrophe. Is it someone's fault? Did they do something wrong? What could they have done differently? What can they do to change the situation?

Your Message

Sometimes the only way to figure out what to do about something is to go over it thoroughly, considering every angle and aspect. You may do this on your own or with others. It has been said that the only way to get the right answer is to ask the right question. If you ask enough questions in relation to your problem, you will eventually find the right answer.

SWORDS

6

6 OF SWORDS

THE TWO FAE have exhausted all possibilities. In the end, they realize that they did not have the wisdom or experience to deal with this situation—but they know someone who does. They decide to seek guidance from their faerie queen. Perhaps she would know what to do to save the magic rosebud and the garden. Too much was at stake for them to deal with this on their own. Although they still feel frightened and alarmed, the decision to take some action—even just asking for help—allows them to feel hopeful. They think they are at last moving in the right direction.

Your Message

Sometimes problems are too big or too complex to face on your own. No matter how many questions you ask or how much you think about it, you can find no answer and can devise no plan. In those cases, you would do well to seek out the advice of someone with the knowledge and experience to help. Deciding to do this may be a small step, but it is a step in the right direction.

7

UPON HEARING HER companions' tale, the queen quickly made her way through the garden and found the dying rosebud. She senses the danger of the situation and fears the worst. She doesn't stop to consider but acts quickly, perhaps too quickly. She pours her faerie magic upon the rosebud and garden. To her delight, the color and scent of the roses return. Suddenly, everything around her begins to grow more and more quickly, and she is unable to stop it. The roses seem almost animated, twisting and turning as they grow larger.

Your Message

Even wise people make mistakes. There is much danger in acting in haste. Be careful of the allure of doing something, anything, to change a situation. Your actions may indeed end the problem, but create an entirely different and perhaps worse problem. No matter how dire the situation, take the time to think before you act.

SWORDS

8

Before the beautiful, beloved queen can fly away, the blood-red thorns wrap themselves around her, binding her to the spot. Her wings and arms are bound behind her, useless. She is immobilized, unable to work any magic; she is entirely defenseless. However, the magic blue bud is beginning to open, so even as her situation seems hopeless, still she has hope that somehow the magic of the rose will save her, the garden, and her people, despite her impulsive act.

Your Message

You may find yourself in a situation where you feel bound, defenseless, and hopeless. You feel trapped, with no way out. Panicking will not help. Instead, take a deep breath, calm down, and look around you. Search for something you can focus on that either will help you get through the experience or will help you get out of the situation. You may be surprised to find that such help is closer than you thought.

9

As THE THORN vines wrap themselves tighter and tighter around the queen, she continues to focus on the beautiful magic rose, knowing that somehow it holds her salvation. The queen grows weaker, yet fights despair with hope. As her valiant efforts wane, a bird swoops down, plucks the rosebud, and flies away. The helpless queen mourns her cruel fate, for she believes that without the magic rose, the garden will continue to grow wild, ending her life and perhaps eventually the lives of her people too.

Your Message

You believe that if a certain event happens, you will be doomed. Your life as you know it will be over, and all happiness will be gone. This belief will probably give you strength and help you fight for something you want very much. However, remember that just because you think something is going to bring certain doom doesn't mean that it will. Fight for what you want, but don't forget that your worst-case scenario may not be as dire as you think.

SWORDS

10

*J*UST AS THE queen thought, throughout the night the vine wrapped tighter about her body and the thorns continued to grow, piercing her delicate skin. Her limp, seemingly dead body is held upright by the very vines that may have killed her. Her blood flows deep red, in stark contrast to the deep green vines and silvery blue blooms. From the spot where her first blood fell, a new little blue rosebud has begun growing. Although the queen cannot see it, it has a wonderful and powerful magic. Behind this tragic scene, the sky is rosy with the promise of sunshine and hope.

Your Message

What you have feared and tried to avoid has happened. Something has ended, and your life is changed—changed but not over. The worst is over, and you may feel exhausted; you may even feel dead inside for a while. But without a doubt, something new will come to fill the empty space, and a new morning will bring the promise of the sunrise and renewed hope.

MORAL

Trying to eliminate all pain from your life will only create bigger problems. Embrace the natural cycles of life, both the joyful and the tragic.

PENTACLES

A
FAERIE'S
FORTUNE

PENTACLES

ACE

ACE OF PENTACLES

Once upon a time, on a fine spring day, there was a young faerie who wandered away from her friends and family, enchanted by the wonders of the woods. She spent the day walking, following whatever path took her fancy. When night fell, she found a comfortable spot and fell asleep. When she woke the next morning, she realized that she was lost. She spent days trying to find her way back home, but never could. She didn't worry too much, though. The quiet beauty of the forest suited her, and there was plenty of food all around her.

After she decided not to try to find her way back home, she spent many happy days enjoying herself. She saw that there was enough bounty around her and that she could make a very nice home. When she lived in the village, she learned how to grow gardens for food and how to weave baskets to store the food for winter. There was

nothing that she couldn't take care of on her
own.

Your Message

You are in the fortunate position of having
enough skill and resources to create the life you
want. You are in a good place that has everything
you need. Look around you and recognize all the
beauty and gifts in your life. Honor these gifts by
expressing your gratitude and by using your skills
to make the most of your opportunity.

2

2 OF PENTACLES

IN HER VILLAGE, the young fae worked alongside others planting
gardens that had been estab-
lished for years. Starting from
scratch was another story. She
had to clear the ground and
gather seeds on her own. Sometimes it was hard
work, and she wondered how she would manage.
But she had no choice, so she did what must be
done. She took the time to weave baskets to help
carry the seeds and to fashion simple tools to dig
in the earth. Being a practical and bright young
fae, she made manageable plans and remembered
to take time out of her days to enjoy the beauty of
nature.

Your Message

You probably feel like you have too much to
do and not enough time to do it in. You are juggling many tasks and have a to-do list that never
seems to end. Help yourself out of the chaos by
prioritizing your projects and jobs. Make sure

you are being as efficient as you can. Don't forget to balance work and pleasure; no life is in balance without both.

3

$\mathcal{H}$ER PLANNING AND juggling of tasks has paid off. The faerie works happily in her garden, planting and tending it. She grows vegetables for food. She also makes room in her garden for whimsical flowers like poppies and daisies, for their beauty and to attract butterflies. The seeds sprout into seedlings that grow into strong plants. Soon, they bear blooms with the promise of food. As the fruit and vegetables grow, she remembers everything she learned about gardening and takes care that they are safe and free of bugs and disease.

Your Message

You have many wonderful skills, and now is the time to put those skills to good use. Work carefully and thoroughly, doing the best that you can. Create things that are useful and things that bring joy to your life. Experience the pleasure of doing something well.

PENTACLES

4

WHILE THE FRUIT and vegetables are ripening, the faerie artistically weaves lovely baskets so she can store her harvest. Autumn is near, and her garden is full of lovely grapes, apples, tomatoes, and other delicious treats. After she has gathered the bounty from her garden and stored it in her baskets, she admires the lush scene. The colors and scents delight her. She anticipates the flavors and textures that will sustain her through the winter. Her long summer of careful work has paid off. She is extremely proud of the result and cannot remember being so happy in her life.

Your Message

It is time to gather the fruits of your labors and plan for the future. You have worked hard and long, and now it is time to reap the benefits. It is also time to make sure you have enough stored to sustain you through the times ahead, which may be lean. Admire and enjoy what you have accumulated, and be grateful for your bounty.

5

𝒯HE FAERIE CANNOT believe what has happened. Rats came, and they stole everything she worked so hard for. They took her fruits and vegetables and trampled her garden. The life she worked so hard to create has been destroyed. Sitting amongst the ruins, she is too devastated to do anything but mourn her loss. She stays there as the weather grows colder, not even noticing her own hunger, growing weaker and weaker. When she tries to think about her future, about what to do during the winter, she is overwhelmed and hopeless. She wonders, almost idly, if she will die.

Your Message

You find yourself in a state of lack—both materially and emotionally. You feel hopeless and worried. Maybe you're too tired to even try to figure out what to do. Your challenge, despite how the situation feels, is to find resources around you that you aren't noticing. Don't let this state overtake you. Don't let yourself become used to this situation. Pull yourself up, and look for a way to improve your circumstance.

6

6 OF PENTACLES

𝒯HE YOUNG FAE, in a very weakened state, is discovered by a family of harvest mice. They see the sad situation she is in and take pity on her. They will not let this poor faerie perish. They bring her fruit and seeds, sharing from their own stores. Their generosity and kindness overwhelm her. She takes their charity graciously and with a very grateful heart. As she regains her strength, she tells them her tale. They invite her to spend the winter with them. They do everything they can to make her feel welcome and let her know that she is not a burden.

Your Message

If you are in a position of need, you will find someone to help you. This generosity may overwhelm you and, at the same time, be hard to accept. It can be difficult to accept help, to think of it as "charity"—as if that is a bad thing. Everyone can use help now and then. If it is there when

6 OF PENTACLES

you need it, accept it gratefully. If you are in a
position to help someone else and choose to do
so, remember that it is hard to accept help, and
try to bestow your help in a way that allows the
recipient to maintain his or her dignity.

PENTACLES

7

SHE GOES WITH the mice to their home. Winter is fast approaching, and there is still much to do to prepare for it. The practical young fae wishes to be useful. She helps to gather the last of the seeds and nuts. She observes their piles of food and sees that they are just that—piles. Knowing that they now have an extra mouth to feed and knowing that proper storage will help the food stay fresher and tastier, she begins to weave baskets designed to store each type of food. The mouse family is duly impressed by her skills and is grateful for her contribution.

Your Message

A situation is approaching that requires careful consideration and planning. As you think about the upcoming situation, make sure that you determine what your needs will be and figure out the best way to meet those needs. A little planning ahead can make the future much easier and more enjoyable. Lack of planning can create unnecessary stress. Why scramble about at the last minute dealing with crises if they can be avoided?

PENTACLES

8

8 OF PENTACLES

THE MICE ARE fascinated by the baskets that the faerie weaves. She sees their interest and offers to teach them how. They watch closely as she shows them how and explains all the tips and tricks that she has learned to make neat, strong, and attractive baskets. They ask her questions about design and construction, things that she never thought about. These questions lead her to come up with new ideas to make better and prettier baskets. The mice also have ideas of their own. They adapt some basket-weaving techniques to their nests and beds, making them sturdier and more comfortable.

Your Message

Now is a time to learn something new ... either brand-new or to challenge yourself by improving something you already know how to do. Or perhaps it is time for you to teach someone else something new. The thing to keep in mind about teaching is that teachers can learn things, too.

PENTACLES

9

HE WINTER DAYS are short, and the winter nights are long. The faerie and the harvest mice spend their long winter nights in exquisite warmth and comfort. Their well-earned sleep is deep and untroubled. They are confident that they made themselves good shelter from the cold and stored up plenty of food for when they wake up. They are all happy that they made good choices through hard times. So they contentedly snuggle together and sleep soundly, enjoying dreams of warm spring days.

Your Message

You have worked hard to create a safe, secure life for yourself. You faced choices that weren't easy. You overcame troubles and misfortune. Sometimes you sacrificed immediate pleasures for the sake of your long-term goals. If you don't have the life you want, realize that you can if you are willing to do what it takes to make it happen.

PENTACLES

10

𝕿HE LONG, COLD winter months are not dreary or boring for the harvest mice and their faerie guest. Every meal is a merry winter feast with tasty food, pleasant company, general good cheer, and a festive party atmosphere. The companions share stories, make plans, and discuss weaving and gardening techniques. They enjoy constant entertainment and help keep each other's spirits up. They all agree it is the most pleasant winter they have ever spent. And truth be told, if they hadn't experienced it themselves, they'd say such domestic bliss was nothing but a faerie tale.

Your Message

You really cannot ask for more: a comfortable home, enough good food, lots of affection, and plenty of good company. You're not bored or lonely. Your life is filled with good things and good people. Enjoy them, and work hard to keep them. If your life isn't filled with good things,

take a close look at your actions and choices.
How have they affected your current situation?
What can you do to change it?

Moral

Having plenty is a good thing.
Having loved ones to share it
with is even better.

CHAPTER 4

The Court Cards

You know that the Major Arcana cards represent milestones or major life events. You've seen that the Minor Arcana show events in everyday life— they set the stage. The only thing missing, really, is people to walk across that stage. That's where the court cards come in. They represent either other people in your life or aspects of yourself. When doing a reading, it is always a good idea to first try to interpret a court card as an aspect of yourself. If that doesn't work in the context of the reading, then it probably represents someone else. Remember that even though the court cards are shown as male or female on the cards, they can represent someone of either gender.

The court cards each have specific characteristics, but each type of card shares some basic traits too, such as:

> KNAVES: students, novices, eager, undisciplined, can represent a message
>
> KNIGHTS: focused, extreme, committed, trained but inexperienced, can represent a fast-moving situation
>
> QUEENS: mature, thoughtful, nurtures individuals
>
> KINGS: mature, likes to organize, manages groups

Each court card belongs to a suit, just like the Minor Arcana, so each court card is concerned with the types of things its suit represents, such as:

WANDS: projects and careers

CUPS: emotions

SWORDS: challenges, ways of thinking

PENTACLES: material resources, making things

Because the court cards represent people (or yourself), they don't bring a specific message to the reading like the Major or Minor Arcana. The court cards—or the people they represent—bring more of an energy to the reading. They are more descriptive than prescriptive. For the same reason, there are no keywords for the court cards in the "Quick Reference Guide" in the back of this book.

KNAVE

THE COURT CARDS

THE KNAVE OF Wands represents someone who has been preparing to try something new. He has studied and observed. He thinks he is ready, but it is important for him to get it right on the first try, so he is imagining exactly what he is going to do. While he prefers action, he dislikes looking like a fool more than he dislikes sitting still, so he will delay action until he is sure he can do something perfectly. Because of this, he may resist taking risks.

He can also represent a message about your career, a project you're working on, or a course of study you are interested in.

WANDS

KNIGHT

THE KNIGHT OF Wands shows a strong, focused warrior. She is filled with disciplined energy and is ready to be given a task. Her passion for action will only be held in check for so long. If she isn't given a task, she will go off and find a quest. She can become restless if sedentary for too long.

WANDS

QUEEN

The Queen of Wands is someone who loves to be involved in grand undertakings. She will help anyone do almost anything, as long as it's not fussy or too detail-oriented. She enjoys the spotlight, so make sure her talent and energy get the praise they deserve. While she does love to help, she'd rather do so by doing something rather than talking, so don't expect her to be a great listener.

WANDS

KING

The King of Wands is an energetic, ambitious leader who thrives on social recognition. He tends to focus on one project at a time to the exclusion of all else. This dedication to a single project can make his life run a bit unbalanced at times. He may tend to forget or neglect other things, such as his family or his physical needs.

KNAVE

THE COURT CARDS

○HE KNAVE OF Cups is generally happy and perhaps a bit naïve regarding the complexities of emotions. She has little experience with tragedy and tends to see things in black and white, and therefore can be judgmental. Despite her lack of experience or depth, she has a good heart and is ready to share that with almost anyone.

She can also represent a message about a romance, an artistic or creative project, or an emotionally charged situation.

KNIGHT

THE KNIGHT OF Cups is dreamy and romantic. She is in love with the idea of being in love. While she may not see things strictly in black and white, she does experience her emotions strongly and extremely. She is interesting to be around, having a flair for the dramatic, but she can be exhausting. Her emotions are usually based more on her whims than on reality.

CUPS

QUEEN

THE QUEEN OF Cups doesn't necessarily love easily, but she does love well. She is creative, thoughtful, and makes an excellent listener—especially if chatting over a rich mocha with delicious cookies on the side, as she is a bit of a sensualist. She loves to help people in emotional crisis but can sometimes be a little controlling or manipulative.

KING

THE KING OF Cups is a compassionate and caring leader. He probably cares more about people's happiness than about efficiency. He would no doubt be happier being a museum curator than head of a financial institution. His love of all things beautiful and his frustrated artistic desires may sometimes distract him from the task at hand.

KNAVE

THE COURT CARDS

THE KNAVE OF Swords is incredibly confident and intelligent. She usually understands the theory behind whatever it is that she wants to do. And to her, that's all you need. If you have an intellectual understanding, why should you not be able to just do something? So she tends to jump right into things, whether or not she's really prepared. Luckily, failure never seems to get her down.

She can also represent a message about a current problem or situation.

KNIGHT

THE KNIGHT OF Swords spent many long hours training her body and disciplining her mind. She will master with precision anything she sets her mind to. Her dedication to her goal will take precedence over everything else, which means other people's needs and emotions may fall victim to her quest.

SWORDS

QUEEN

HE QUEEN OF Swords has known sorrow and survived it. It has made her strong and smart. It has also made her a little distant and perhaps a little cold. Like all the Queens, she is creative and tends to excel in complex, intricate forms of artistic expression—such as playing the harp. She has a natural wit and way with words, so she is great company. But she won't suffer fools easily. However, she is a great source of no-nonsense wisdom and advice. She'll no doubt have the easiest and surest solution to a problem, but she may deliver her gems with a sharp tongue.

KING

THE COURT CARDS

$\mathcal{T}$HE KING OF Swords defines himself as rational. He is. He can go into a disaster zone and have a new city built before someone else even organizes a cleanup crew. He can win a chess tour-nament, direct a battle, or take over a company. He's efficient and effective. Doing something and doing it well are more satisfying to him than any public or private recognition. While his intellec-tual needs are huge, his emotional needs appear to be minimal. Or are they?

KNAVE

THE COURT CARDS

𝒯HE KNAVE OF Pentacles is able to enjoy the good things of life without much care. She finds joy in simple pleasures. Not one to overcomplicate matters, she takes things as they are. She enjoys experimenting and making things, and she loves to share the things she has made. While she always completes her projects, she doesn't necessarily master them before moving on to something else. Because she is quiet, some may think she lacks depth or intelligence.

She can also indicate a message about a project, money, resources, or health.

PENTACLES

KNIGHT

ᏅHE KNIGHT OF Pentacles has a deep love and respect for things of beauty. Not necessarily quick to action, he spends time pondering the value of things and ideas. Once he has decided their merit, he dedicates himself to their protection. He can be trusted to keep things (material goods, people, secrets) safe. Uninterested in going off and pursuing new activities, some may think him dull, but his devotion knows no equal.

PENTACLES

QUEEN

HE QUEEN OF Pentacles is the quintessential artist or craftsperson. She is the perfect balance of technical skill and creative innovation. Whatever she tries, you can be certain she will be good at it. And she will try lots of things. When she finds the thing that delights her hands and enchants her imagination, then she will be brilliant. She is not averse to public recognition of her talents, and her accomplishment may blind her to the needs of others.

KING

THE KING OF Pentacles throws the best parties and is the perfect host. He always goes to great lengths to provide the best for his guests. While he will never be the life of the party himself, he'll make sure that everyone has a good time. He has worked hard to enjoy the pleasures of life, and nothing makes him happier than to share these things with those he loves. He may neglect his intellectual or emotional well-being.

CHAPTER 5

Visiting the Faerie Garden

THE *Mystic Faerie Tarot* is more than a collection
of beautiful images that tell charming tales. It is a
tool to help you find your own way through the
garden of your life. Use this tool by performing a
reading. A reading is made up of several steps:

1. Creating a sacred space.

2. Asking a question.

3. Selecting a spread.

4. Shuffling the cards.

5. Laying out the cards.

6. Interpreting the reading.

7. Thanking the faeries for their help.

8. Cleansing and storing your cards.

We'll go through each of these steps, so you know exactly what to do to get the clearest answers.

Creating a Sacred Space

When performing a reading, you are seeking spiritual guidance from the faerie realm. To help promote good communication between yourself and the fae, make a doorway of sorts through which you can invite the faeries to share their wisdom. Also, you'll be more focused and ready to receive the message if you prepare yourself and your space.

How you create the space and prepare yourself can be as simple as clearing a flat surface to lay the cards on and taking a few deep breaths to center yourself. Many people use more elaborate rituals. Consider the following ideas and see if any seem right for you.

- Use a special cloth to lay your cards on. A plain cloth is preferred, as a patterned cloth may distract you from focusing on the card's images. A cloth defines your space and helps keep your focus on the reading.

- Light a pink or white candle to invite positive energy into your space or a blue one to promote clarity.

- Burn incense such as lemongrass, which aids in psychic ability, or lavender or rosemary, which invite loving energy into the space.

- Place a crystal or gem in your space. If you are seeking answers pertaining to love, use a rose quartz. If you are exploring a question that is difficult or scary, tiger's-eye has a protective quality, and amethyst promotes courage.

- Ground and center yourself: place your feet flat on the floor, relax, close your eyes, and breathe deeply three times.

- Say a prayer or simply invite the fae into your space.

Asking a Question

If you are looking for the right answers, you'd better ask the right questions. Remember, predicting the future is a lot like predicting the weather. The future is not entirely predetermined. While we can see how a certain set of events will lead to a probable outcome, things can happen to suddenly change the course of events. And of course, just as with a weather prediction, the further into the future you look, the less clear the picture is.

To use these cards most effectively, it is best to ask questions that help you understand either the current situation or past events that created the current situation and that help you decide your best course of action for the future. While there are things in your life that you cannot control, there are many more that you do control. Focus on those aspects, and take a proactive approach to life—it is, after all, your life. Here are a few examples:

> LESS EFFECTIVE: Will I find true love soon?
> MORE EFFECTIVE: What can I do to bring more love into my life?

LESS EFFECTIVE: Will my financial situation improve?

MORE EFFECTIVE: How can I improve my financial situation?

There are, naturally, aspects and events you cannot control. But you can decide how best to react to these events. The cards can be helpful in these cases as well. Again, how you approach the question is very important. For example:

LESS EFFECTIVE: My company downsized, and I lost my job. What am I going to do?

MORE EFFECTIVE: My company downsized, and I lost my job. What new opportunities are before me?

LESS EFFECTIVE: My father recently passed away. When will the pain end?

MORE EFFECTIVE: My father recently passed away. What do I need to do to heal?

Once you've decided on your question, write it down to help maintain your focus as you interpret the reading.

Selecting a Spread

A spread is a diagram that tells you how to lay out the cards and what each position means. The meaning of the position affects how you interpret the card. If this sounds a little confusing, don't worry. There are examples of how to do this later.

You'll find a collection of spreads here. In addition, there are lots of books of spreads and even spreads available on the Internet. Usually there is a sentence or two that tells what type of question the spread was designed to answer. Look over the spreads available, read the description, and look at the position meanings. By doing that, you can usually tell if a spread is right for your question.

Don't feel like you have to use a predesigned spread. If you want, you can design a spread yourself to answer a specific question.

Shuffling the Cards

You can shuffle your cards any way you like. Some people like to make shuffling part of their beginning ritual. For example, shuffle the deck the same number of times for each reading, or after shuffling, divide the deck into three piles, and then pick them back up in a different order.

However you do it, always remember that as you are shuffling, focus on your question, and invite faerie wisdom to direct the shuffling.

Laying Out the Cards

The spread you select will tell you in what order and in what positions to lay the cards. You have to decide two things.

First, how will you pick the cards to lay? After shuffling, you can simply deal the cards off the top. Or you can spread them out (facedown!), and pick them randomly one by one.

Second, will you lay the cards faceup or facedown? It is suggested that you lay the cards faceup, so you can see the spread as a whole before beginning to read each card. Later, when we discuss interpreting the reading, you'll see how useful this can be. However, you can, if you wish, lay the cards facedown, and flip them over one at a time as you interpret them. This increases the sense of mystery and allows you to focus on each card as it is revealed.

Interpreting the Reading

Assuming you've laid your cards faceup, the first thing you'll do is survey the reading as a whole using the following tips:

1. If there are a predominance of Major Arcana cards (more than one-third of the cards in the spread), then this reading has a special significance. Perhaps it holds a deeper spiritual meaning, indicates a major life change, or indicates more events than usual beyond your control.

2. If there are many court cards (more than one-fourth of the cards in the spread), then either other people or several aspects of your personality are involved.

3. If there is a majority of one suit over the others, then consider the following:

   a. Wands = work or projects; watch for lots of fast-moving energy in this situation (especially if there is a knight in the spread)

   b. Cups = love, relationships, or emotions dominating the situation

   c. Swords = problems, challenges; the way you think about things has much influence in the situation

   d. Pentacles = money, health, resources, or finishing something are the focus in this situation

4. The numbered cards can play a role independent of their suit.

   a. If there are several aces, 2s, or 3s, then the situation is at its beginning

   b. If there are several 4s, 5s, or 6s, then the situation is in the middle

   c. If there are several 7s, 8s, or 9s, then the situation is nearing resolution

   d. If there are 10s, the situation is nearly over, and a new one is developing (especially if there is also an ace in the spread)

5. Sometimes during shuffling, some cards may become turned upside down. When you lay them down, they appear upside down in relation to the other cards. Tarot readers call this a "reversed" card. In the

VISITING THE FAERIE GARDEN

Mystic Faerie Tarot, reversed cards are ones that the faeries want you to pay special attention to.

After you've done your survey, go through each card one by one. First, look at the image, and see what meaning you find there. Listen and hear whether there is a special message beyond that of the written meaning. Second, look up the card meaning (if necessary), and think about it in relation to its position in the spread. Finally, consider the message of the card in terms of the question. Using this process, you should be able to interpret each card as part of the answer to your question. After you've done this for each card, put it all together to find your answer.

Many people find it helpful to write down their readings as they go along, especially if there are more than three cards involved. As you can see, you can get a lot of information out of just one card. The more cards in the spread, the more details you have to keep track of.

Thanking the Faeries for Their Help

After your reading, thanking the fae for their guidance is a good idea, especially if you plan on asking for it again in the future!

Cleansing and Storing Your Cards

After doing a reading, you may want to cleanse your cards before doing another reading or before putting them away. You can do this any number of ways.

1. Put all your cards upright and in order.

2. Pass the cards through the smoke of burning sage.

3. Store them with a rose or clear quartz.

This next idea isn't always practical, but it's great for inviting faerie energy into your readings. Set your deck on a windowsill (inside!) in the light of a full moon for one night.

CHAPTER 6

Spreads

1

Dew Drop

Some of the smaller faeries use drops of dew as a mirror. This single-card reading works as a mirror. Simply ask: "What do I need to know about _____?" or "What do I need to know today?" Pull a single card and get a quick answer.

SPREADS

Lily Pond

Lily ponds have magical qualities that provide clarity and insight. This simple three-card spread will help you see a situation with more clarity as well as provide insight regarding the possible future.

1. PAST: events or actions in the past that made the foundation for the current situation

2. PRESENT: what is happening right now

3. FUTURE: based on past events and the current situation, what the probable future is

Hint: if you are unsatisfied with the final card, do another reading. For example, if you want to alter the future, try the Acorn to Oak spread (page 262), or if you want to understand why you don't like the probable future, try a Nighttime Forest Stroll (page 264).

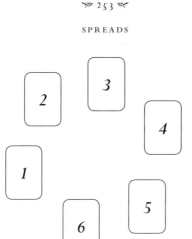

Faerie Ring

To do this reading, divide your cards into six stacks—one stack of the Major Arcana and one each of the Swords, Cups, Wands, Pentacles, and all the court cards. Shuffle each stack separately. Take each stack and place it as directed below:

1. Major Arcana

2. Wands

3. Cups

4. Swords

5. Pentacles

6. Court Cards

Faeries gather in a ring to dance and celebrate. After they are gone, toadstools grow in a ring where they danced. In this spread, you will discover aspects of yourself that you should celebrate and aspects of yourself that you might want to improve.

These cards represent the best and strongest aspects of your personality. Value them, and use them to make your life everything you've dreamed of.

Turn up the top card on each stack, and interpret them as follows:

1. Your greatest spiritual strength

2. Your most enterprising characteristic

3. Your best emotional strength

4. Your strongest response to problems

5. Your most admirable financial/resource ability

6. Your favorite aspect of your personality

After that, take the card from the bottom of each pile, lay it crossways on top of the top card, and interpret it as follows:

1. Your most important spiritual challenge at this time

2. Your most problematic attitude toward work

3. Your most difficult emotional challenge at this time

4. Your worst fear when facing problems

5. Your financial weakness

6. Your least favorite aspect of your personality

These cards show the parts of yourself you are least happy with. Once you understand them, you are well on your way to improving them and your life.

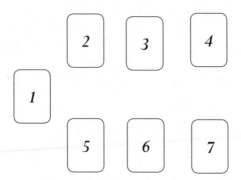

Two Paths in the Garden

Just like coming to a fork in a garden or woodland path, life is filled with multiple paths. When you are faced with a choice between two paths, use this spread to help you decide which to take. If you are faced with more than two choices, simply alter this spread by adding more paths.

1: What you need to know about where you are right now

2 and 5: These are the benefits of each path

3 and 6: These are the downsides of each path

4 and 7: These are the probable outcomes of each path

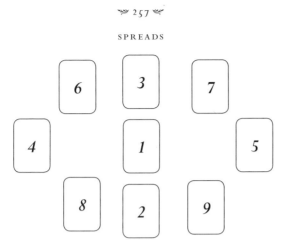

Love Me, Love Me Not Daisy Spread

You've heard of plucking off daisy petals to determine if he "loves you" or "loves you not." That tradition inspired this spread but examines the question a little differently. It focuses more on how *you* feel about the relationship. You'll be able to see your current relationship more clearly and find ways to improve it.

1. What you need to know about how you see this relationship

2. The strongest aspect or foundation of this relationship

3. What you hope for in this relationship

4. What happened in the past that is affecting this relationship

5. What you can expect from this relation-ship

6. Your favorite thing about this relationship

7. What you can do to make your favorite thing even better

8. Your least favorite thing about this relationship

9. What you can do to improve your least favorite thing

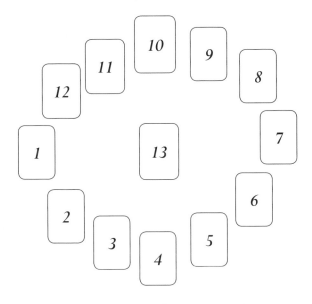

Your Birthday Sunflower Spread

Every year, the sun returns to the same place it was when you were born. Because of that, the sunflower is an apt symbol for a birthday. This is a great reading to do every year on your special day to get some insight into what your year ahead holds in a variety of areas. It is based on the charts used to do astrological readings.

13. What you need to know right now

1. Your self-image and personality

2. Your value systems and material resources

SPREADS

3. Your siblings and communication

4. Your parents, your home and family

5. Creativity, affairs of the heart, fun, and children

6. Work, responsibilities, and health

7. Partnerships (romantic and business)

8. Sex, death, and other people's money

9. Travel, higher education, spiritual connections

10. Your public image, vocation, and ambition

11. Friends, hopes, goals, and wishes

12. Your inner self, dreams, secrets, the past

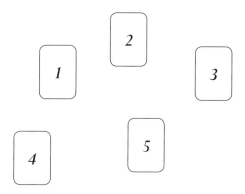

Rose Petals

Roses are forever linked with love and romance. This spread is designed to help you draw love into your life.

1. This is something nice you need to do for yourself

2. This is something you need to learn

3. This is an issue you need to address

4. This is a step you can take to find love

5. This is a goal you need to work toward

SPREADS

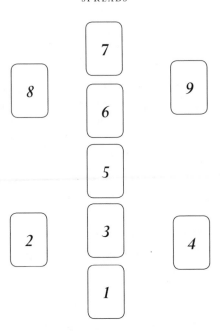

Acorn to Oak

Mighty oaks grow from tiny acorns. You can help your dreams—any dreams, whether they are about love, money, family, your home, a vacation—become reality. Use this spread to make it happen. This one works a little differently than most because you use the cards faceup to pick the first and the seventh cards. First, look through your cards and select one that best depicts your goal—this is your oak and will be placed in the seventh position. Then, look through your cards

again and pick a card that best represents where
you are right now in relation to your goal. This
is your acorn and will be placed in the first position. The rest of the cards are shuffled and laid
out as usual; they will tell you what you need to
do to achieve your goal and what you can expect
along the way.

1. YOUR ACORN: where you are now

2. SOIL: what resources you need to get
   started

3. SUNSHINE: what you need to know to
   help it grow

4. WATER: what you need to do to nurture it
   along

5. KNOT: what unexpected delay you can
   plan for and maybe circumvent

6. TRUNK: what will help you be strong

7. YOUR OAK: your goal

8. BRANCHES: benefits of your oak

9. LEAVES: unexpected gifts from your oak

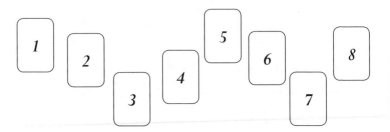

A Nighttime Forest Stroll

Walking through a forest at night can be a beautiful, mystical experience. But if it is a large and unfamiliar forest, it can be a little scary, because you don't know where things are, and the moonlight can create illusions that throw you off. When you are facing something that frightens or upsets you, it can be like walking through such a forest. Your mind can play tricks on you, making things into something they are not. This spread can help you identify what is frightening you, what part of that fear is real, and what part is an illusion of the moonlight. Knowledge is power, and this spread will empower you to face your fears.

SPREADS

1. What you need to know most about what you fear

2. What aspect of your fear is real

3. How you can combat it

4. What aspect of your fear is an illusion

5. How you can banish the illusion

6. What you fear the most

7. How you can overcome it

8. What you will learn by overcoming this fear

CHAPTER 7

Sample Readings

Darcy at Work

Darcy has to make a presentation at work. She was recently promoted, and this is her first presentation. She is nervous and excited. She turns to the faerie garden for some guidance, using the Dew Drop spread.

> QUESTION: What do I need to know to make a good impression during my presentation?

> CARD: Wheel of Fortune

> INTERPRETATION: Darcy's message is that her attitude is key. She shouldn't focus on the

presentation as a big, scary event to be overcome. Instead, it is an opportunity to be confident, practice her presenting skills, and illustrate
her knowledge. As long as she is prepared and
knows what she is doing, the situation—whether
a formal presentation, a meeting with execu-
tives, or a call to a client—doesn't matter. She
knows what she is doing and will handle herself
with aplomb.

Megan and Dating, Part 1

Megan, a woman in her early twenties, just
ended a long-term relationship. Well, really, her
boyfriend ended it. She feels adrift and unsettled
and really wants to be in another relationship.
She decides to be proactive and is determined to
find true love. She asks out Joe, whom she has
met a few times through a co-worker. The date is
approaching, and Megan wants to know what to
expect—might this be "the one"? She selects the
Lily Pond spread to find out.

THE QUESTION: What can I expect from my
date with Joe?

Past: 2 of Swords

Present: Knight of Cups reversed

Future: Knight of Wands

Megan notices immediately the two knights, so she knows that things will happen fast, and that makes her pretty happy … at first.

As she interprets the spread more closely, she sees:

> Past (2 of Swords): She has made a conscious choice to start dating, with the goal of finding her true love.

> Present (Knight of Cups reversed): Since this card is reversed, she pays close attention to it. Its meaning of being in love with love and having romantic notions based on, well, romance, rather than reality, bothers her. Is she really like that?

> Future (Knight of Wands): This card says that she will pursue the relationship too determinedly—that she might lose sight of other things she should be paying attention to.

This reading makes Megan think about what she is after and question her motives. Her last relationship ended because he thought she was too committed too early. And here she was again, wondering the same thing about someone she hadn't even had one date with. Not wanting to make the same mistakes again and not liking the possible future shown here, she decides to do the Acorn to Oak reading.

Megan and Dating, Part 2

There is no doubt in her mind: Megan does want love. Who doesn't? And there's nothing wrong with that. But what does she need to do to really experience it, not just force it into being? Using the Acorn to Oak spread to find out, she chooses the Knight of Cups as her Acorn, representing her current dreamy-love self, and selects the Lovers to illustrate her goal—to be ready for love and to make good choices.

1. HER ACORN: Knight of Cups

2. SOIL: 2 of Pentacles

3. SUNSHINE: 2 of Wands

4. WATER: 2 of Cups

SAMPLE READINGS

5. KNOT: The Devil

6. TRUNK: 7 of Pentacles

7. HER OAK: The Lovers

8. BRANCHES: The Priest

9. LEAVES: The Hermit reversed

Scanning her reading, she is really amazed to see that all the cards that have to do with getting the seed growing are twos ... things at the beginning of something and usually having to do with choices or commitment. She is a little afraid of the Knot being the Devil. But the top row is all Major Arcana cards; that's got to be promising.

1. HER ACORN, WHERE SHE IS NOW (KNIGHT OF CUPS): She already knows this: she has unrealistic expectations and is in love with the idea of love.

2. SOIL, WHAT SHE NEEDS TO DO TO GET STARTED (2 OF PENTACLES): She needs to prioritize. She needs to first get herself ready for a relationship before she pursues one.

3. SUNSHINE, WHAT SHE NEEDS TO KNOW TO HELP IT GROW (2 OF WANDS): She needs to

make a commitment to herself to follow through with her plan, no matter what might distract her.

4. WATER, WHAT SHE NEEDS TO DO TO NUR-TURE THE SEED (2 OF CUPS): If she does date Joe, or anyone else, she needs to enjoy the early stages of a relationship for what they are. She should focus on getting to know the person and having fun and letting love unfold.

5. KNOT, AN UNEXPECTED DELAY (THE DEV-IL): She needs to remember that she is try-ing to end a pattern of behavior and that won't come easy just because she decides to change. Her old habit of defining her-self by her relationship may try to get in the way.

6. TRUNK, WHAT WILL HELP HER BE STRONG (7 OF PENTACLES): She can plan for the Knot—her old habits—by maintaining her sense of self and making sure she has a full life aside from her dating life. She can make sure she has plenty of plans with friends and family so she isn't tempted to

spend all her time with whomever she is dating.

7. HER OAK, THE GOAL (THE LOVERS): Through a process of sound choices, she will discover herself and be happier with herself. Then she'll have more to offer a partner and will probably enjoy a more satisfying relationship.

8. BRANCHES, THE BENEFITS (THE PRIEST): She should focus on developing herself and learning. Taking classes or committing to volunteer work will strengthen who she is.

9. LEAVES, UNEXPECTED GIFTS (THE HERMIT REVERSED): This one is the biggest surprise to Megan. Who would have thought that the goal of being with someone else would have the benefit of being alone? Since it is reversed, she knows to not just write this card off. Through the process of becoming herself, of learning about who she is, she will learn to be fulfilled on her own, so ironically, the need to be in a relationship will be less driving for her.

Moving Day for Kelli

Kelli has always lived in New York. On a whim, she interviewed for a job in Seattle. To her surprise, she was offered the job. While it's not necessarily a "dream" job, it is pretty good. The pay beats anything she'd get in New York, it is definitely a step up from her current job, and the company offers great benefits. At this point in her life, there is no reason why she shouldn't take it, except one: moving across the country, leaving friends and family, is, let's face it, a scary proposition. Exciting, yes, but also a little overwhelming. Kelli takes a Nighttime Forest Stroll with her *Mystic Faerie* cards to see what happens.

The Spread

> QUESTION: What am I so afraid of regarding moving to Seattle?

1. What does she need to know the most about her fear? 7 of Wands.

2. What aspect of her fear is real? 8 of Pentacles.

3. How can she combat it? The World.

4. What aspect of her fear is an illusion? Wheel of Fortune reversed.

5. How can she banish the illusion? Temperance.

6. What does she fear most? 3 of Swords reversed.

7. How can she overcome it? Queen of Cups.

8. What will she learn by overcoming this fear? The Lovers.

The Interpretation

1. WHAT DOES SHE NEED TO KNOW THE MOST ABOUT HER FEAR? (7 OF WANDS): The 7 of Wands is about a disagreement in a partnership. But her fear, this move, has nothing really to do with anyone else, so it is about her and her fear. It is holding her to a sort of agreement to stay in New York. It allows no compromise. She either lives with it in New York or confronts it and is free to go where she wants. Or stay, if she chooses to. That's the main difference, choosing to stay out of reasons other than fear.

SAMPLE READINGS

2. WHAT ASPECT OF HER FEAR IS REAL? (8 OF PENTACLES): Wow, this is almost embarrassing. The part of her fear that is real is that she'd have to learn new things, like how to get around a new city, where to shop, and how to find new friends. For a bright, independent young woman, who'd think that'd be scary?

3. HOW CAN SHE COMBAT IT? (THE WORLD): This one is almost embarrassing, too, in its obviousness. Kelli decides to read this one literally. That is, combat the fear of learning a new city by the reality of the excitement of exploring the world.

4. WHAT ASPECT OF HER FEAR IS AN ILLUSION? (WHEEL OF FORTUNE REVERSED): It's reversed, so Kelli knows to pay extra attention to this one. It's about things constantly changing but staying true to yourself and centered. She's lived in the same place for so long, and so little has changed. She has defined herself in terms of New York. Will she lose her sense of who she is if New York isn't the center of her life?

SAMPLE READINGS

5. How can she banish the illusion? (Temperance): Huh. Both these cards are about being centered, about being sure of who she is. They both say to be yourself no matter what is going on around you.

6. What does she fear most? (3 of Swords reversed): Another reversed card, and probably the one that hits closest to home. It's all about being afraid that she'll be so heartbroken and so homesick that she won't even be able to function in her new job, her new environment, her new life—that she will return to New York as a failure.

7. How can she overcome it? (Queen of Cups): Interesting. This card describes Kelli already. It's true, she is a bit of a sensualist. That's why she loves New York—there is so much to see and do and experience. The other two cards counseled her to be herself. What she fears the most is failing. So this card says she can overcome her fear of failing by being herself? Kelli thinks she gets it: if she wants to go, she can go. If she doesn't like it, she can come

back. Success is about finding what makes her happy, even if she has to try a few different things to know. Success isn't about getting it perfect the first time out.

8. WHAT WILL SHE LEARN BY OVERCOMING THIS FEAR? (THE LOVERS): Will she meet her soulmate in Seattle? Possibly. But more probably what she'll learn is how to make this and other decisions based on reasons other than fear.

QUICK REFERENCE GUIDE

MAJOR ARCANA

0, THE FOOL: Follow your dreams

1, THE MAGICIAN: Use your talents wisely

2, THE PRIESTESS: Live your values

3, THE EMPRESS: Nurture with love, not control

4, THE EMPEROR: Serve the greater good

5, THE PRIEST: Pursue higher knowledge

6, THE LOVERS: Choose wisely and love deeply

7, THE CHARIOT: Take control

8, STRENGTH: Wield power gracefully

9, THE HERMIT: Challenge your beliefs

QUICK REFERENCE GUIDE

10, WHEEL OF FORTUNE: Choose your reactions wisely

11, JUSTICE: Choose your actions wisely

12, THE HANGED FAE: Sacrifice and faith

13, DEATH: Acceptance and hope

14, TEMPERANCE: Center yourself and seek balance

15, THE DEVIL: Choose your pleasures carefully

16, THE TOWER: A belief is destroyed

17, THE STAR: Renewal and guidance

18, THE MOON: Lovely dreams and dangerous illusions

19, THE SUN: Happiness and joy

20, JUDGEMENT: Heed a higher calling

21, THE WORLD: Completion of a great task

WANDS

ACE: Adventure

2: Partnership

3: Opportunity

4: Prosperity

5: Challenge

6: Victory

7: Defiance

8: Swiftness

9: Resilience

10: Burden

Cups

ACE: New love

2: Commitment

3: Celebration

4: Boredom

5: Sorrow

6: Memories

7: Choices

8: Seeking

9: Fulfillment

10: Contentment

Swords

Ace: Problem

2: Protection

3: Heartache

4: Rest

5: Discussion

6: Decision

7: Haste

8: Restriction

9: Cruelty

10: Hope

Pentacles

Ace: Foundation

2: Balance

3: Skill

4: Possessions

5: Poverty

6: Generosity

7: Planning

8: Learning

9: Comfort

10: Wealth

GET MORE AT LLEWELLYN.COM

Visit us online to browse hundreds of our books and decks, plus sign up to receive our e-newsletters and exclusive online offers.

- Free tarot readings • Spell-a-Day • Moon phases
- Recipes, spells, and tips • Blogs • Encyclopedia
- Author interviews, articles, and upcoming events

GET SOCIAL WITH LLEWELLYN

Find us on   @LlewellynBooks

www.Facebook.com/LlewellynBooks

GET BOOKS AT LLEWELLYN

LLEWELLYN ORDERING INFORMATION

Order online: Visit our website at www.llewellyn.com to select your books and place an order on our secure server.

Order by phone:
- Call toll free within the U.S. at 1-877-NEW-WRLD (1-877-639-9753)
- Call toll free within Canada at 1-866-NEW-WRLD (1-866-639-9753)
- We accept VISA, MasterCard, American Express and Discover

Order by mail:
Send the full price of your order (MN residents add 6.875% sales tax) in U.S. funds, plus postage and handling to: Llewellyn Worldwide, 2143 Wooddale Drive Woodbury, MN 55125-2989

POSTAGE AND HANDLING

STANDARD (U.S. & Canada):
(Please allow 12 business days)
$30.00 and under, add $4.00.
$30.01 and over, FREE SHIPPING.

INTERNATIONAL ORDERS:
$16.00 for one book, plus $3.00 for each additional book.

Visit us online for more shipping options. Prices subject to change.

FREE CATALOG!

To order, call
1-877-
NEW-WRLD
ext. 8236
or visit our
website

The Llewellyn Tarot

Anna-Marie Ferguson

From the creator of the popular *Legend: The Arthurian Tarot Kit,* this lavishly illustrated deck offers universal appeal (based on Rider-Waite) with a Welsh twist. A compelling story unfolds starring Rhiannon as the Empress, Bran the Blessed as the Emperor, the Wild Herdsman as the Horned God (the Devil), Gwydion as the Magician, Llew Llaw Gyffes as the Bringer of Light, and other figures from Welsh mythology. Watercolor imagery beckons us forth into a mystic world of ancient forests, sensuous seascapes, and wondrous waterfalls—gorgeous landscapes brimming with mystery, meaning, and magic. Also included is *The Llewellyn Tarot Companion,* which features an introduction to the craft and history of tarot, along with Welsh legends infused in this deck.

978-0-7387-0299-5

Boxed kit includes 78-card deck and 288-page book

The Gilded Tarot

Ciro Marchetti

Companion book by Barbara Moore

A classic tarot deck that dazzles! Heralding archetypal elements of traditional tarot, *The Gilded Tarot* is teeming with shimmering, classic imagery. High priestesses in flowing robes, wise emperors, knights on majestic steeds, mystics wielding magical tools, and other intriguing characters from medieval times abound in the Major and Minor Arcanas. This richly colored, easy-to-use deck also features standard symbols for the card suits—swords, cups, wands, and pentacles—which provides universal appeal.

This kit also includes *The Gilded Tarot Companion,* a clear and insightful guidebook to the deck's structure and each card's significance.

978-0-7387-0520-0

Boxed kit includes 78-card deck and 192-page book